THE HISTORIC REALITY
OF CHRISTIAN CULTURE

In a work of broad scope, Professor Dawson defines the basic elements of culture—a common way of life, a tradition embodied in institutions, moral standards and principles. He discovers in the interaction of Christianity and Western civilisation throughout the ages a definite cycle of of historic action: an age of intense spiritual activity in response to a new historical situation, a period of achievement in which new forms of life, art and thought are created, and time of retreat when the Church is attacked from within or without.

THE AUTHOR

Christopher Dawson is Stillman-Guest Professor of Roman Catholic Theological Studies at Harvard University. Among his many books are *Religion and Culture*, *Christianity and the Rise of Western Culture* and *Dynamics of World History*.

THE HISTORIC REALITY
OF CHRISTIAN CULTURE

A Way to the Renewal of Human Life

RELIGIOUS PERSPECTIVES
Planned and Edited by
RUTH NANDA ANSHEN

THE
HISTORIC REALITY
OF
CHRISTIAN CULTURE

A Way to the Renewal of Human Life

by Christopher Dawson

LONDON

Routledge and Kegan Paul Ltd.

First published in England 1960
by Routledge & Kegan Paul Ltd.
Broadway House, 68-74 Carter Lane,
London, E.C.4
Printed in Great Britain
by Lowe & Brydone (Printers) Ltd.,
London, N.W.10

CONTENTS

RELIGIOUS PERSPECTIVES
Its Meaning and Purpose

RELIGIOUS PERSPECTIVES represents a quest for the rediscovery of man. It constitutes an effort to define man's search for the essence of being in order that he may have a knowledge of goals. It is an endeavor to show that there is no possibility of achieving an understanding of man's total nature on the basis of phenomena known by the analytical method alone. It hopes to point to the false antinomy between revelation and reason, faith and knowledge, grace and nature, courage and anxiety. Mathematics, physics, philosophy, biology and religion, in spite of their almost complete independence, have begun to sense their interrelatedness and to become aware of that mode of cognition which teaches that "the light is not without but within me, and I myself am the light."

Modern man is threatened by a world created by himself. He is faced with the conversion of mind to naturalism, a dogmatic secularism and an opposition to a belief in the transcendent. He begins to see, however, that the universe is given not as one existing and one perceived but as the unity of subject and object; that the barrier between them cannot be said to have been dissolved as the result of recent experience in the physical sciences, since this barrier has never existed. Confronted with the question of meaning, he is summoned to rediscover and scrutinize the immutable and the permanent which constitute the dynamic, unifying aspect of life as well as the principle of differentiation; to reconcile identity and diversity, immutability and unrest. He begins to recognize that just as every person descends by his particular path, so he is able to ascend, and this ascent aims at a return to the source of creation, an inward home from which he has become estranged.

It is the hope of RELIGIOUS PERSPECTIVES that the rediscovery of man will point the way to the rediscovery of God. To this end a rediscovery of first principles should constitute part of the quest. These principles, not to be superseded by new discoveries, are not those of historical worlds that come to be and perish. They are to be sought in the heart and spirit of man, and no interpretation of a merely historical or scientific universe can guide the search. RELIGIOUS PERSPECTIVES attempts not only to ask dispassionately what the nature of God is, but also to restore to human life at least the hypothesis of God and the symbols that relate to him. It endeavors to show that man is faced with the metaphysical question of the truth of religion while he encounters the empirical question of its effects on the life of humanity and its meaning for society. Religion is here distinguished from theology and its doctrinal forms and is intended to denote the feelings, aspirations and acts of men, as they relate to total reality.

RELIGIOUS PERSPECTIVES is nourished by the spiritual and intellectual energy of world thought, by those religious and ethical leaders who are not merely spectators but scholars deeply involved in the critical problems common to all religions. These thinkers recognize that human morality and human ideals thrive only when set in a context of a transcendent attitude toward religion and that by pointing to the ground of identity and the common nature of being in the religious experience of man, the essential nature of religion may be defined. Thus, they are committed to re-evaluate the meaning of everlastingness, an experience which has been lost and which is the content of that *visio Dei* constituting the structure of all religions. It is the many absorbed everlastingly into the ultimate unity, a unity subsuming what Whitehead calls the fluency of God and the everlastingness of passing experience.

These volumes will seek to show that the unity of which we speak consists in a certitude emanating from the nature of man who seeks God and the nature of God who seeks man. Such certitude bathes in an intuitive act of cognition, participating in the divine essence and is related to the natural spirituality of intelligence. This is not by any means to say that there is an equivalence of all faiths in the traditional religions of human history. It is, however, to emphasize the distinction between the spiritual and the temporal which all religions acknowledge. For duration of thought is composed of instants superior to time, and is an intuition of the permanence of existence and its metahistorical reality. In fact, the symbol* itself found on cover and jacket of each volume of RELIGIOUS PERSPECTIVES is the visible sign or representation of the essence, immediacy and timelessness of religious

* From the original design by Leo Katz.

experience; the one immutable center, which may be analogically related to Being in pure act, moving with centrifugal and ecumenical necessity outward into the manifold modes, yet simultaneously, with dynamic centripetal power and with full intentional energy returning to the source. Through the very diversity of its authors, the Series will show that the basic and poignant concern of every faith is to point to, and overcome the crisis in our apocalyptic epoch—the crisis of man's separation from man and of man's separation from God—the failure of love. The authors will endeavor, moreover, to illustrate the truth that the human heart is able, and even yearns, to go to the very lengths of God; that the darkness and cold, the frozen spiritual misery of recent time, are breaking, cracking and beginning to move, yielding to efforts to overcome spiritual muteness and moral paralysis. In this way, it is hoped, the immediacy of pain and sorrow, the primacy of tragedy and suffering in human life, may be transmuted into a spiritual and moral triumph.

RELIGIOUS PERSPECTIVES is therefore an effort to explore the *meaning* of God, an exploration which constitutes an aspect of man's intrinsic nature, part of his ontological substance. The Series grows out of an abiding concern that in spite of the release of man's creative energy which science has in part accomplished, this very science has overturned the essential order of nature. Shrewd as man's calculations have become concerning his means, his choice of ends which was formerly correlated with belief in God, with absolute criteria of conduct, has become witless. God is not to be treated as an exception to metaphysical principles, invoked to prevent their collapse. He is rather their chief exemplification, the source of all potentiality. The personal reality of freedom and providence, of will and conscience, may demonstrate that "he who knows" commands a depth of consciousness inaccessible to the profane man, and is capable of that transfiguration which prevents the twisting of all good to ignominy. This religious content of experience is not within the province of science to bestow; it corrects the error of treating the scientific account as if it were itself metaphysical or religious; it challenges the tendency to make a religion of science—or a science of religion—a dogmatic act which destroys the moral dynamic of man. Indeed, many men of science are confronted with unexpected implications of their own thought and are beginning to accept, for instance, the trans-spatial nature of events within spatial matter.

RELIGIOUS PERSPECTIVES attempts to show the fallacy of the apparent irrelevance of God in history. The Series submits that no convincing image of man can arise, in spite of the many ways in which human thought has tried to reach it, without a philosophy of human nature and human freedom which does not exclude God. This image of *Homo cum Deo* implies the highest conceivable freedom, the freedom to step into the very fabric of the universe, a new formula for man's collaboration with the creative process and the only one which is able to protect man from the terror of existence. This image implies further that the mind and conscience are capable of making genuine discriminations and thereby may reconcile the serious tensions between the secular and religious, the profane and sacred. The idea of the sacred lies in what it *is,* timeless existence. By emphasizing timeless existence against reason as a reality, we are liberated, in our communion with the eternal, from the otherwise unbreakable rule of "before and after." Then we are able to admit that all forms, all symbols in religions, by their negation of error and their affirmation of the actuality of truth, make it possible to experience that *knowing* which is above knowledge, and that dynamic passage of the universe to unending unity.

The volumes in this Series will seek to challenge the crisis which separates, to make reasonable a religion that binds and to present the numinous reality within the experience of man. Insofar as the Series succeeds in this quest, it will direct mankind toward a reality that is eternal and away from a preoccupation with that which is illusory and ephemeral.

For man is now confronted with his burden and his greatness: "He calleth to me, Watchman, what of the night? Watchman, what of the night?"[1] Perhaps the anguish in the human soul may be assuaged by the answer, by the *assimilation* of the person in God: "The morning cometh, and also the night: if ye will inquire, inquire ye: return, come."[2]

RUTH NANDA ANSHEN

[1] Isaiah 21:11.
[2] *Ibid.,* 21:12.

New York, 1960

THE HISTORIC REALITY
OF CHRISTIAN CULTURE

A Way to the Renewal of Human Life

1
The Outlook for Christian Culture

THERE IS ALWAYS A DANGER IN SPEAKING OF SO wide and deep a question as that of Christian culture that we may be speaking at cross-purposes. It is therefore just as well to start by defining our terms. When I speak of culture I am not thinking of the cultivation of the individual mind, which was the usual sense of the word in the past, but of a common social way of life—a way of life with a tradition behind it, which has embodied itself in institutions and which involves moral standards and principles. Every historic society has such a culture from the lowest tribe of savages to the most complex forms of civilized life. And every society can lose its culture either completely or partially, if it is exposed to violent or far-reaching changes.

What then do we mean by a Christian culture? In fact the word Christian is commonly used in two different senses. There is a sense in which it is identified with certain forms of moral behavior which are regarded as typically or essentially Christian, so that a Christian society may mean an altruistic and pacific society, and an unchristian society or form of behavior is taken to mean one that is aggressive and acquisitive.

Whether this use of the word is justifiable or not, it is certainly different from the traditional use of the word. Thus if we judge by the utterances of statesmen and the programs of governments and political parties, there has never been an age in which society has concerned itself more with the welfare and conditions of life of the common people than our own. Yet though this concern is wholly consonant with Christian ideals and may even owe its ultimate inspiration to them, it does not suffice to make our society Christian in a real sense; and the tendency to put exclusive emphasis on this aspect of the question will be a serious cause of error, if it leads us to a confusion of Christianity with humanitarianism.

The only true criterion of a Christian culture is the degree in which the social way of life is based on the Christian faith. However barbarous a society may be, however backward in the modern humanitarian sense, if its members possess a genuine Christian faith they will possess a Christian culture—and the more genuine the faith, the more Christian the culture.

And so when we talk of Christian culture, we ought not to think of some ideal pattern of social perfection which can be used as a sort of model or blueprint by which existing societies can be judged. We should look first and above all at the historic reality of Christianity as a living force which has entered into the lives of men and societies and changed them in proportion to their will and their capacity. We see how it has been spread broadcast over the world by the grace of God and the accidents of historical necessity. Often it has fallen on stony ground and withered away, often it has been choked by the secular forces of a civilization, but where it has taken root, we see again and again the miracle of divine creativity and a new spiritual harvest springing from the old soil of human nature and past social tradition.

This flowering of new life is Christian culture in the highest sense of the word, but every believing Christian society already has in it a living seed of change which is bound to bear fruit in due time, even if its growth is hidden or hindered by the many other growths which are so deeply rooted in the soil of human nature that they can never be eradicated. We cannot measure spiritual achievement by cultural achievement, since the two processes lie on different planes; but though the former transcends the latter it may also find in it its means of expression and outward manifestation. But there is always a time lag in this process. The spiritual achievement of today finds its social expression in the cultural achievements of to-morrow, while today's culture is inspired by the spiritual achievement of yesterday or the day before.

If we take the case of the first introduction of the Christian faith in Europe, we see how complex and profound is the process that we are attempting to understand. When St. Paul sailed from Troy in obedience to a dream and came to Philippi in Macedonia, he did more to change the course of history and the future of European culture than the great battle which had decided the fate of the Roman Empire on the same spot more than ninety years before. Yet nothing that he did was notable or even visible from the standpoint of contemporary culture. He incurred the hostility of the mob, he was sent to prison and he made at least three converts: a business woman from Asia Minor, a slave girl who was a professional for-tuneteller, and his jailer. These were the first European Christians—the forerunners of uncounted millions who have regarded the Christian faith as the standard of their European way of life.

All this took place, as it were, underneath the surface of culture. The only people who seem to have realized the im-portance of what was happening were the half-crazed slave girl and the hostile mob at Philippi and Salonica, the riffraff of the market place, who attacked St. Paul as a revo-lutionary, one who turned the world upside down and taught there was another king than Caesar—one Jesus.

Yet at the same time St. Paul himself was very much alive to the significance of culture. He was a Roman and a Jew and he was proud of both traditions; but he was always careful to adapt his teaching to the cultural background of his audience, whether they were simple, peasant-minded Anatolians or skeptical Athenians or supercilious Roman administrators. So that when one turns from St. Paul's own utterances to the writings of his learned contemporaries, one feels that one is going down in the cultural scale, descending from a rich and vivid vision of reality to a stale and superficial repetition of platitudes and rhetorical commonplaces which belonged to a spiritual order that had already lost its vitality.

At first sight the problem of modern culture is entirely different from that of the Roman world. The latter was living in the tradition of the pagan past, and Christianity came to it as a new revelation and the promise of new life. But today it is Christianity that seems to many a thing of the past, part of the vanishing order of the old Europe, and the new powers that are shaping the world are non-Christian or even anti-Christian.

It is no wonder that the conscience of Christians is uneasy. On the one hand there are those who still retain an internal bond with the Christian culture of the past, and a deep love and reverence for it; and in that case they must feel that something in the nature of a national apostasy has occurred and that they bear some share of the guilt. And on the other hand there are those who have lost contact with that social tradition and who know only the new secularized world. These are likely to feel that the Christian culture of the past failed because it was not really Christian and that it is for us and our successors to discover or create for the first time a new way of life that will be truly Christian.

I believe both these points of view are fundamentally true. They represent the two aspects of the problem of Christian culture in our time, and they are wrong only in so far as they are one-sided. I do not think it is possible to deny the fact of

Christian culture, as an objective social reality. It is hardly too much to say that it is Christian culture that has created Western man and the Western way of life. But at the same time we must admit that Western man has not been faithful to this Christian tradition. He has abandoned it not once, but again and again. For since Christianity depends on a living faith and not merely on social tradition, Christendom must be renewed in every fresh generation, and every generation is faced by the responsibility of making decisions, each of which may be an act of Christian faith or an act of apostasy.

No doubt it is very seldom that a society is clearly conscious of what is at stake. The issues are complicated by all kinds of social, economic and political influences, so that the actual decision usually takes the form of a compromise.

Now, as I have pointed out with reference to the origins of Christianity, the creative activity which is the essence of the Christian life takes place far below the visible surface of culture; and the same thing is true of the spiritual failures and apostasies which are the other side of the picture. But this does not mean that religion and culture are two separate worlds with no relation to each other. The assumption of such a separation has been the great error of the Western mind during the last two centuries. First we have divided human life into two parts—the life of the individual and the life of the state—and have confined religion entirely to the former. This error was typical of bourgeois liberalism and nowhere has it been more prevalent than in the English-speaking countries. But now men have gone further and reunited the divided world under the reign of impersonal material forces, so that the individual counts for nothing and religion is viewed as an illusion of the individual consciousness or a perversion of the individual craving for satisfaction.

This is the typical error of Marx and Engels and of the totalitarian mass state in all its forms.

B

But to the Christian the hidden principle of the life of culture and the fate of nations and civilizations must always be found in the heart of man and in the hand of God. There is no limit to the efficacy of faith and to the influence of these acts of spiritual decision which are ultimately the response of particular men to God's call, as revealed in particular historical and personal circumstances. Burke wrote very truly and finely that the so-called laws of history which attempt to subordinate the future to some kind of historical determinism are but the artificial combinations of the human mind. There always remains an irreducible element of mystery. "A common soldier, a child, a girl at the door of an inn have changed the face of the future and almost of Nature."

But to Christians the mystery of history is not completely dark, since it is a veil which only partially conceals the creative activity of spiritual forces and the operation of spiritual laws. It is a commonplace to say that the blood of martyrs is the seed of the Church, yet what we are asserting is simply that individual acts of spiritual decision ultimately bear social fruit. We admit this in the case of the Church and we have admitted it so long that it has become a platitude. But we do not for the most part realize that it is equally true in the case of culture and history.

For the great cultural changes and the historic revolutions that decide the fate of nations or the character of an age are the cumulative result of a number of spiritual decisions—the faith and insight, or the refusal and blindness, of individuals. No one can put his finger on the ultimate spiritual act which tilts the balance and makes the external order of society assume a new form. In this sense we may adapt Burke's saying and assert that the prayer of some unknown Christian or some unrecognized and unadmitted act of spiritual surrender may change the face of the world.

No doubt any great change of culture, like the conversion

of the Roman world or the secularization of Western Christendom, is a process that extends over centuries and involves an immense variety of different factors which may belong to different planes of spiritual reality. The secularization of Western Christendom, for example, involved first the loss of Christian unity, which was itself due not to secularism but to the violence of religious passion and the conflict of rival doctrines. Secondly it involved the abdication by Christians of their responsibilities with regard to certain fields of social activity, so that we may say that nineteenth-century England was still a Christian society, but a Christian society that had diverted its energies to the pursuit of wealth. And finally it involved a loss of belief, which was to a certain extent involuntary and inevitable, since the stability of faith had already been undermined by the two processes which I have mentioned.

To state the problem in a simplified form, if one century has destroyed the unity of Christendom by religious divisions, and a second century has confined the Christian way of life to the sphere of individual conduct and allowed the outer world of society and politics to go its own way, then a third century will find that the average man will accept the external social world as the objective standard of reality and regard the inner world of faith and religion as subjective, unreal and illusory.

Thus the process of secularization arises not from the loss of faith but from the loss of social interest in the world of faith. It begins the moment men feel that religion is irrelevant to the common way of life and that society as such has nothing to do with the truths of faith. It is important to distinguish this secular separation between religion and society from the traditional opposition between the Church and the World—or between the present world and the world to come—which has always been so deeply rooted in the Christian tradition. It is often difficult thus to differentiate, since what is described as the "other-worldly" type of religion is in some cases directly connected with the divorce between religion and culture of which I have spoken. In other cases the opposition springs from the Christian dualism which finds expression not only in St. Augustine, or in the later mystics, but in all ages of the life of the Church from the New Testament to the twentieth century. Indeed it is this vital tension between two worlds and two planes of reality which makes the Christian way of life so difficult but which is also the source of its strength. To live for eternal truths, to possess the first fruits of eternal life, while facing every practical responsibility and meeting the demands of the present moment and place on their own ground—that is the spirit by which a Christian culture lives and is known. For Christian culture involves a ceaseless effort to widen the frontiers of the Kingdom of God—not only horizontally by increasing the number of Christians but vertically by penetrating deeper into human life and bringing every human activity into closer relations with its spiritual center.

The return from a secular civilization to a Christian way of life no doubt involves a reversal of many historical forces that transcend the limits not only of our personal experience but even of our particular society. But in spite of the modern totalitarian tendency to control the development of culture by the external methods of legislation and international organization and the control of parties and political police, it is still the individual mind that is the creative force which determines the ultimate fate of cultures. And the first step in the transformation of culture is a change in the pattern of culture within the mind, for this is the seed out of which there spring new forms of life which ultimately change the social way of life and thus create a new culture. I do not, of course, mean to assert that new ideas are more important than new moral action and new spiritual initiative. Knowledge and will and action are inseparable in life, and the soul is the principle of all life. But I do believe that it has been on the plane of ideas that the process of the secularization of culture began, and that it is only by a change of ideas that this process can be reversed. It has always been the weakness of the Anglo-Saxon tradition to underestimate the influence of ideas on life and of contemplation on action, and the result of this error has been that many Christians in England and America never realized the existence of culture until the culture of the age had ceased to be Christian.

That was the situation a hundred years ago. It is true that there were several religious minority movements that were aware of the issues—on the one hand the Christian Socialists, such as F. D. Maurice; on the other hand, there was the idealization of the ages of faith which characterized the Catholic revival and the Oxford Movement. But for the most part Victorian England was dominated by that attitude of Protestant Philistinism which was the object of Matthew Arnold's denunciations. Now it is true, as Mr. T. S. Eliot has recently pointed out, that Arnold's view of culture is vitiated not only by its individualism but even more seriously by its implicit assumption that intellectual culture is itself a sort of sublimated religion which is a substitute for traditional Christianity. But, for all that, he still deserves to be read, for no one has shown more clearly and mercilessly the effects of the divorce between religion and culture on English society and the English way of life; and since our present predicament is the direct result of this cleavage, his work is a historical document of the first importance for the inner history of the English culture of the nineteenth century.

Moreover, Arnold's main criticism of the religion of his day is not invalidated by his misconceptions concerning the nature of religion and the nature of culture. The burden of his complaints is always that *religious people would not think*—that they made religion a matter of strong emotion and moral earnestness so that it generated heat and not light. And that at the same time they were complacent and uncritical in their attitude to their own bourgeois culture: so long as men went to church and read the Bible and abstained from gambling and drunkenness and open immorality, it did not matter that they were at the same time helping to turn England into a hideous and disorderly conglomeration of factories and slums in which the chapel and the gin palace provided the only satisfaction for man's spiritual and emotional needs.

The reaction against this degradation of Christian culture has carried us very far in the opposite direction. And the improvement of social conditions—one might almost say the civilizing of our industrial society—has coincided with the secularization of English culture.

This secularization has been the great scandal of modern Christendom. For the Christian cannot deny the crying evils of that nineteenth-century industrial society from which the ordinary man has been delivered by the social reforms of the last fifty or one hundred years: while at the same time he is forced to reject the purely secular idealism which has inspired the new culture. Nevertheless this has been a salutary experience for Christians. It has made us examine our conscience to see how great has been our responsibility for this decline of Christian culture and for the conversion of our society to a new kind of paganism.

But we ought not to concentrate our attention on the failures of nineteenth-century Christianity. Today we are faced with a new situation and an entirely different range of problems. The modern world is in a state of violent confusion and change, and it is not the traditional Christian culture of the past but the secularized culture of the present which is being tried and found wanting. The material security and the confidence in the future which have long been characteristic of Western civilization have suddenly disappeared. Nobody knows where the world is going. The course of history has suddenly been changed from a broad, placid river into a destructive cataract.

Christianity is not left unaffected by this change, for it threatens all the values and traditions which the liberal secularism of the last age still respected and preserved. Yet this catastrophic element in life which had been temporarily exiled from the nineteenth-century world is one that is very familiar to Christians. Indeed, in the past it formed an integral part of the original Christian experience and the changes of the last forty years have confronted us with a situation which is not essentially different from that the primitive Church faced under the Roman Empire. The eschatological aspect of Christian doctrine, which was so alien to the Edwardian age, has once more become relevant and significant. For even though we may not believe in the imminent end of the world, it is hardly possible to doubt that *a* world is ending. We are once more in the presence of cosmic forces that are destroying or transforming human life, and therefore we have a new opportunity to see life in religious terms and not merely in terms of humanism and social welfare and political reform. Arnold's ideal of culture as a "general harmonious expansion of those gifts of thought and feeling which make the peculiar dignity, wealth and happiness of human nature" obviously belonged to an age and a class which could reckon on social security. For that age the four last things—Death and Judgment and Heaven and Hell—had become remote and unreal. But today they are real enough even for the unbeliever who knows nothing of the Christian hope of eternal life. The Christian way of life has indeed become the only way that is capable of surmounting the tremendous dangers and evils that have become a part of the common experience of modern man. No doubt, as the Gospel says, men will go on eating and drinking and buying and selling and planting and building, until the heaven rains fire and brimstone and destroys them all. But they do this with only one part of their minds; there is another part of their minds which remains uneasily conscious of the threat that hangs over them; and in proportion as they realize this, they feel that something should be done and they seek a way of salvation, however vaguely and uncertainly.

In a sense this has always been so, and men have always been partially conscious of their spiritual need. But there has been during the last generation a fundamental change in the nature of their anxiety. During the last few centuries the appeal of Christianity has been largely personal. It has been an appeal to the individual conscience and especially to the isolated and introverted types. It is the experience which finds a classical expression in Bunyan's *Pilgrim's Progress,* which is all the more classical because it was also popular. But today the appeal is greatest to those who have the strongest sense of social responsibility, and it is no longer merely a question of individual salvation but of the salvation of the world—the deliverance of man in his whole social nature from the evils that express themselves in political and social forms, in anonymous mass crimes and criminal instincts which nevertheless are not less opposed to the Christian spirit than are the sins of the individual. This is the reason why the chief rivals to Christianity at the present time are not different religions but political ideologies like Communism, which offers man a social way of salvation by external revolution, by faith in a social creed and by communion with a party which is a kind of secular church.

Nor is it surprising that these secular counter-religions should tend to produce the very evils from which men are seeking to be delivered. For this is just what the early Church experienced with the pagan counter-religions which tried to satisfy the spiritual needs of the ancient world in opposition to the Christian way of salvation.

And the anti-Christian character of the forces which are making an attempt to conquer the world is also another sign of the relevance of Christianity to the problems of the present age. Religion is ceasing to be a side issue—it is no longer regarded as belonging to a private world remote from the real world of business and politics and science. It is once more felt to be a vital issue even by its enemies who are determined to destroy it.

Consequently, in spite of the increasing secularization of culture both in the West and in the world at large, I feel that the outlook for Christian culture is brighter than it has been for a considerable time—perhaps even two hundred and fifty years. For if what I have been saying about spiritual changes and their cultural fruits is true and if the changes of the last forty years have the effect of weakening the barrier between religion and social life which was so strong a century ago, then the new situation opens the way for a new Christian movement of advance.

This is no excuse for facile optimism. For even if the change has begun, it must go a long way before it can affect the structure of social life and bear fruit in a living Christian culture: and meanwhile things must grow worse as secular culture undergoes the inevitable process of corruption to which it is exposed by its nature. From all that we can see, and from the experience of the past, it is practically certain that the period of transition will be a time of suffering and trial for the Church. Above all we have little or no knowledge of how Christians are to meet the new organized forces with which they are confronted. However much these forces may have misused the new techniques that science has put into their hands, these techniques cannot be ignored and they are bound to become an integral part of the civilization of the future, whether it is Christian or anti-Christian. So long as it is only a question of material techniques—of the machine order and all that it implies—Christians are ready enough to accept the situation, perhaps almost too ready. But what of the social and psychological techniques on which the totalitarian state relies and which may almost be said to have created it? All these methods of mass conditioning, social control by centralized planning, the control of opinion by propaganda and official ideologies, the control of behavior by methods of social repression are not restricted to defending society from the evil-doer but are directed against any type of minority opinion or activity. Most of these things have been rejected and condemned by Western opinion, whether Christian or secular, yet many of them are already invading and transforming Western society, and they are likely to become more and more a part of the modern world. Seen from this point of view, the Nazis and the Communists are not the only totalitarians, they are only parties which have attempted to exploit the totalitarian elements in modern civilization in a simplified and drastic way in order to obtain quick results.

The whole tendency of modern life is toward scientific planning and organization, central control, standardization and specialization. If this tendency was left to work itself out to its extreme conclusion, one might expect to see the state transformed into an immense social machine, all the individual components of which are strictly limited to the performance of a definite and specialized function, where there could be no freedom because the machine could only work smoothly so long as every wheel and cog performed its task with unvarying regularity. Now the nearer modern society comes to this state of total organization, the more difficult it is to find any place for spiritual freedom and personal responsibility. Education itself becomes an essential part of the machine, for the mind has to be as completely measured and controlled by the techniques of the scientific expert as the task which it is being trained to perform.

Therefore the whole society has to move together as a single unit. Either it may be a Christian unit which is governed by spiritual standards and directed toward spiritual ends, or it is wholly secular—a power machine, or a machine for the production of wealth or population.

As I have said, this is an extreme conclusion, and at the present time even the most totalitarian forms of society are not and cannot be as totalitarian as this. Nevertheless the modern world is moving steadily in this direction, and the margin between the old forms of liberal or social democracy and this new Leviathan is growing narrower every year. Hence we can hardly doubt that when ultimately a conflict takes place between the new state and the Christian church, it will be far more severe in character than anything that has been known before.

Here again the trend of events is following the same pattern as in the early days of Christianity. Nothing was clearer to the Christians of that age than the imminence of a tremendous trial, in which the mystery of iniquity that was already at work in the world would come out into the open and claim to stand in the place of God Himself. It was with the constant awareness of this coming catastrophe that the new Christian way of life took form, and it was this that made the Christian belief in a new life and in the coming of a new world, not an expression of other-worldly pietism, but an active preparation for vast and immediate historical changes. There is no need to idealize their behavior. At times the actual outburst of persecution was followed by wholesale apostasies, as in the time of Decius in the year 250. Yet in spite of such failures, throughout the long periods of persecution and semipersecution a gradual change was taking place beneath the surface until finally, after the last and fiercest persecution of all, the world suddenly awoke to find that the Empire itself had become Christian.

We today are living in a world that is far less stable than that of the early Roman Empire. There is no doubt that the world is on the move again and that the pace is faster and more furious than anything that man has known before. But there is nothing in this situation which should cause Christians to despair. On the contrary it is the kind of situation for which their faith has always prepared them and which provides the opportunity for the fulfillment of their mission.

It is true that we do not know where the world is going. We cannot say it must go toward a Christian culture any more than toward destruction by atomic warfare. All we know is that the world is being changed from top to bottom and that the Christian faith remains the way of salvation: that is to say, a way to the renewal of human life by the spirit of God which has no limits and which cannot be prevented by human power or material catastrophe. Christianity proved victorious over the pagan world in the past, because Christians were always looking forward while the secular world was looking back. This note of hope and expectation is one of the characteristic notes of Christianity: it runs through the New Testament from beginning to end. One of the most striking expressions of this is to be seen in St. Paul's last letter to his first European converts—the Philippians—written during his captivity and trial, yet making even his trial a ground of encouragement, since it was providing a means to spread the knowledge of the faith in the Roman prætorium and the palace of Caesar. And after describing all his gains and all his losses, he concludes:

"Not that I have already reached fulfillment. I do not claim to have attained. But this one thing I do. Forgetting all that is completed and reaching out to the things that lie before,

I press on to the goal for the prize of the high calling of God in Christ Jesus."

This attitude of detachment and confidence in the future which St. Paul expresses in such an intensely personal, vivid way is also the social attitude of the Church as a whole, and it is this which gives Christianity such a great power of spiritual renewal.

Nevertheless, though Christianity is prepared to accept every external change, though it is not bound to the past in the same way as a particular form of society tends to be, it has its own internal tradition which it maintains with the most scrupulous fidelity and which it can never surrender. Looked at from the secular standpoint, the primitive Church might have seemed to lack everything that the educated Roman regarded as culture. Yet in reality it was the representative of a cultural tradition older than that of Greece and Rome. To the Christian, the people of God was a real historical society with its own history and literature and its perennial philosophy of divine wisdom. And when eventually the world became Christian, this specifically religious culture-tradition came to the surface and was accepted by the new world as the source of the new Christian art and literature and liturgy.

The same tradition exists today, for though the Church no longer inspires and dominates the external culture of the modern world, it still remains the guardian of all the riches of its own inner life and is the bearer of a sacred tradition. If society were once again to become Christian, after a generation or two or after ten or twenty generations, this sacred tradition would once more flow out into the world and fertilize the culture of societies yet unborn. Thus the movement toward Christian culture is at one and the same time a voyage into the unknown, in the course of which new worlds of human experience will be discovered, and a return to our own fatherland—to the sacred tradition of the Christian past which flows underneath the streets and cinemas and skyscrapers of the new Babylon as the tradition of the patriarchs and prophets flowed beneath the palaces and amphitheaters of Imperial Rome.

2
What is
a Christian Civilization?

THE QUESTION WHICH I HAVE TAKEN AS THE
title for the present chapter is one of the vital questions of our
times. It is very necessary that we should ask it, yet the fact
that we are doing so is a symptom of the state of doubt and
uncertainty in which modern man exists. For in the past it
was no problem to the ordinary man. Everyone thought—
however mistakenly—that he knew what Christian civilization
was; no one doubted that it was possible; and most people
would have said that it was the only form of civilization possible for Western man.

This was true of the whole Christian world down to the
eighteenth century, and the fact that I can use this expression
—the Christian world—and assume that the reader will know
what I mean is sufficient in itself to prove the point. No doubt
after the eighteenth century this was no longer the case on the
European continent, and there the concept of Christian civilization had already become a controversial one. But this
change did not occur to anything like the same degree in
England and America. The Anglo-Saxon missionary movement of the nineteenth century, for example, as represented by
men like David Livingstone, seems to have taken for granted
that the expansion of Christianity was inseparable from the
expansion of Western civilization. In the eyes of such men

Western civilization was still a Christian civilization as compared with pagan barbarism and the non-Christian civilizations
of the ancient peoples.

It is easy enough for us today to realize their mistake and
to see its tragic consequences. But the danger today is that we
should go to the opposite extreme by denying the social or
cultural significance of Christianity. A man like Livingstone
could not have done his work without the Christian background in which he had been bred. He was the offspring of
a Christian society and a Christian society involves a Christian
culture. For however widely one separates the Word and the
World, Christian faith and secular activity, Church and State,
religion and business, one cannot separate faith from life or
the life of the individual believer from the life of the community of which the individual is a member. Wherever there
are Christians, there must be a Christian society, and if a
Christian society endures long enough to develop social traditions and institutions, there will be a Christian culture and
ultimately a Christian civilization.

But perhaps I have gone too far in assuming general agreement in the use of terms which are by no means so clear as
they appear at first sight. For words like "civilization," "culture," and "Christian" are all of them likely to become highly
charged with emotional and moral associations. I mean that
the word "Christian" is used or was used in the recent past
in the sense of morally excellent; "civilization" usually involved
a judgment of value and implies a very high type of social and
intellectual development; while "culture" is used in two quite
different senses but usually implies a rather sophisticated type
of higher education.

But for the purposes of the present discussion I shall attempt
to use these words in a purely descriptive way, without imply-
ing moral judgments—that is to say, judgments of value. I
use the word "culture" as the social anthropologists do, to

describe any social way of life which possesses a permanent institutional or organized form, so that one can speak of the culture of a tribe of illiterate cannibals. And I use the word "civilization," of any culture that is sufficiently complex to have developed cities and states. Similarly, when I speak of individuals or societies as Christian, I mean that they profess the Christian faith or some form of Christian faith, and not that they are men or peoples who behave as we believe Christians ought to behave.

Let us start at the beginning and inquire what culture—any culture, even the lowest—involves. No culture is so low as to be devoid of some principle of moral order. Indeed, I think we may go further than that and say that a culture is essentially a moral order and this is just what makes it a culture. Even those sociologists who are most inclined to minimize or deny the spiritual element in culture and to view it in a purely behavioristic fashion, like the late Professor W. G. Sumner, are ready to admit that a culture is essentially a system or pattern of "folkways" or "mores" and their use of this Latin term points to a fundamental agreement in the conception of culture. For the word "mores" means morals as well as manners, and though we today make a sharp distinction between ethics and customs, the distinction is a very recent one. The Romans themselves, who were exceptionally aware of ethical problems and possessed a genuine moral philosophy, still had only one word for the two concepts, so that while to the Roman *"boni mores"* had come to mean what we call "good morals," it was also used indifferently to describe good manners. Even today we cannot ignore the close relationship and parallelism between moral education and training in good manners, so that children do not distinguish very clearly between the guilt of a moral offense and the shame of a breach of good manners.

Now when we come to primitive societies, we cannot expect

C

to find any clear distinction such as we take for granted between ethics and customs. But this does not mean that ethics
are less important; on the contrary, they cover a much wider
field and extend further in both directions, inward to religion
as well as outward to society. For in all primitive cultures,
ethics are related to a whole series of concepts which are now
distinguished from one another, but which formerly constituted
different provinces of one moral kingdom, and embraced law
and religious rites as well as morals and social customs. Take
the case of law: the distinction between the moral and the
legal codes is relatively modern, not only in simple cultures
but even in the great historic civilizations of the ancient world.
For the great legal codes were all-inclusive and possessed a
sacred character which conferred the same ultimate sanctions
on the precepts which we should regard as secular, public
or political as on those which seem to us moral or religious or
ceremonial.

This unification of standards is familiar to us historically in
the case of the Hebrew Torah: here the unity of religion,
ethics, law, rites and ceremonies is peculiarly clear and we see
how this sacred law is also regarded as the foundation of the
national culture and the very essence of the people's being.
But there is a similar relation between religion, law, morals
and rites, in the great world cultures of China and India and
Islam no less than in the more primitive cultures.

In China, for example, we see how the Confucian ethics
have been the moral foundations of Chinese culture for more
than two thousand years, so that it is impossible to understand
any aspect of Chinese history without them. They were linked
on the one hand with Chinese religion and ritual, and on the
other with the Chinese political and social order. And they
were also inseparably connected with Chinese education and
the Chinese tradition of learning. Seen in this light, Chinese

culture is an indivisible whole—a web of social and moral relations woven without seam from top to bottom.

We are now in a better position to understand what Christian civilization means. For in the past Christianity has played the same part in Western civilization as Confucianism did in China or Islam in the Middle East. It was the principle of moral unity which gave the Western peoples their spiritual values, their moral standards, and their conception of a divine law from which all human laws ultimately derive their validity and their sanction. Without Christianity there would no doubt have been some kind of civilization in the West, but it would have been quite a different civilization from that which we know: for it was only as Christendom—the society of Christian peoples—that the tribes and peoples and nations of the West acquired a common consciousness and a sense of cultural and spiritual unity. This is not just the theory of a Christian apologist. It is admitted just as much by historians who have no sympathy with Christianity. Edward Gibbon, for example, was notoriously hostile to the whole Christian tradition. Yet he never denied that the Church was the maker of Europe and he concludes his highly critical survey of Christian origins by showing how religious influences and "the growing authority of the Popes cemented the union of the Christian republic; and gradually produced the similar manners and the common jurisprudence which has distinguished from the rest of mankind the independent and even hostile nations of modern Europe."[1]

But when Gibbon speaks of "manners" we must understand it in the extended sense which I have been discussing. For what distinguished the new Christian peoples of Europe from their pagan ancestors was their acceptance of a new set of moral standards and ideals. No doubt their adhesion to these

[1] *Decline and Fall,* ch. XXXVII, ii, "The Conversion of the Barbarians."

new standards was very imperfect in practice, but the same thing was probably true of their old standards, for there is always a considerable gap between the moral standards of a society and the moral practice of individuals, and the higher the standards, the wider the gap; so that we should naturally expect the contrast between moral principles and social behavior to be much wider in the case of Christianity than in a pagan society. Nevertheless, this does not mean that moral and spiritual values are socially negligible. They influence culture in all sorts of ways—through institutions and symbols and literature and art, as well as through personal behavior. Take for example the case of the transformation of the barbarian king or war leader by the sacramental rite of consecration as practiced throughout Europe in the Middle Ages. This obviously did not convert the ordinary feudal monarch into a St. Louis or a King Alfred, but it did establish an ideal norm by which rulers were judged and which moralized the institution itself. And the same is true of the institution of knighthood, and still more true of essentially Christian institutions, like priesthood and episcopacy and monasticism. A Christian civilization is certainly not a perfect civilization, but it is a civilization that accepts the Christian way of life as normal and frames its institutions as the organs of a Christian order. Such a civilization actually existed for a thousand years more or less. It was a living and growing organism—a great *tree of culture* which bore rich fruit in its season. As I say, it was by no means a perfect civilization. In its origins, it was a civilization of converted barbarians and it retained certain barbaric elements which reasserted themselves again and again in the course of its history.

Now our modern Western civilization in Europe and America is the direct successor and heir of this Christian civilization. Without the latter, it would never have existed. Nevertheless, our modern civilization is not a Christian one. It is the result of two hundred years of progressive secularization during which the distinctively Christian institutions and social standards have been gradually eliminated. This process was a complex one. On the continent of Europe, especially in France, it was a violent and catastrophic change, which involved political revolutions and religious persecutions. In England on the other hand it was extremely gradual and piecemeal and even today some of the typical institutions of the old Christian order, like the State establishment of the national Church and the solemn religious consecration of the monarch, still survive. The case of America, or rather of the United States, differs from each of these types. It was the first country in the Christian world to inaugurate the complete separation of the State from the Church. But this did not at first involve the secularization of culture. Throughout the greater part of the nineteenth century it was the churches rather than the State that were responsible for education and culture, especially in the newly settled territories of the Middle and Far West. The complete secularization of public education is a relatively recent factor; so that its impact on American culture has only recently been fully realized.

Thus in all Western lands the outcome of the last two hundred years' development has led to similar results. The traditional Christian civilization has now become a part of history and can only be understood by a considerable effort of study and imagination, while the whole Western world is coming to share a common secular technological civilization which it has transmitted and is in the course of transmitting to the rest of the world—to the old civilizations of Asia and to the new peoples of Africa and Oceania. Yet this secularized civilization both in Europe and America still bears marks of its Christian origins and contains living Christian traditions and institutions, though these are, so to speak, scattered and no longer integrated into the organic structure of the civilization.

Opinions differ as to the relative importance of these elements, according to the personal experience of the individual. As far back as the end of the eighteenth century there were localities and social strata in which the Christian religion was no longer practiced, while there are other regions where it is still accepted today as the basis of social life and education. And it is this broken pattern of Christian culture which is the source of most of our practical difficulties in finding clear answers and satisfactory solutions to the problem that we are discussing. On the one hand we have the point of view presented by Mr. T. S. Eliot in his thoughtful and provocative studies in Christian culture.

In the first of them, *The Idea of a Christian Society,* he writes:

> A society has not ceased to be Christian until it has become positively something else. It is my contention that we have today a culture which is mainly negative, but which in so far as it is positive, is still Christian. I do not think that it can remain negative, because a negative culture has ceased to be efficient in a world where economic as well as spiritual forces are proving the efficiency of cultures which, even when pagan, are positive; and I believe the choice before us is between the formation of a new Christian culture and the acceptance of a pagan one. Both involve radical changes; but I believe that the majority of us, if we could be faced immediately with all the changes which will only be accomplished in several generations, would prefer Christianity.[2]

Now though I naturally agree with Mr. Eliot about the choice we should make, I think he underestimates the degree

[2] *The Idea of a Christian Society* (New York: Harcourt, Brace and Co., 1939), p. 13.

to which modern civilization has acquired a positively secularized character and I am doubtful whether the majority of
modern men are unwilling to accept this state of things. Christian civilization was inaugurated by the acceptance of the
Cross as the Standard—*In hoc signo, vinces.* But modern
civilization has adopted a different standard and it is the sign
of the dollar rather than the cross that now marshals the forces
of Western civilization. I do not think that the majority of
men are unwilling to accept this new standard. The dollar is
a very good thing in its way and there are many good Christians who are quite ready to make it the standard of our civilization. It is true that they do not fully realize what the total
secularization of our civilization would mean. They are ready
to accept a secular state and secular education, but they still
hope to maintain Christian ethical standards and they do not
understand how deeply and in how many ways the spirit of a
civilization influences the moral values of its individual members.

No doubt in the past it has proved possible for churches
and other minority groups to maintain their ethical standards
against those of the dominant culture. But they paid a high
price for this. In the case of the early Christians it meant a
fight to the death between the Church and the pagan world,
in which Christianity triumphed only after long centuries of
persecution. In the case of the Jews in Europe, it has meant
the life of the ghetto and the cramping and impoverishment
of their culture; and in the case of the minority groups in the
modern Christian world, like the Mennonites and the Quakers,
it produced a somewhat parallel phenomenon in the form of
sectarianism which sets the group apart from the wider national culture.

Now if it were possible to preserve the Christian standards
in the life of the family and the religious group, it might well
be worth paying the price, even if it meant a certain loss of

social advantages. But in the highly organized life of the modern secular state it is becoming increasingly difficult for such separate groups to exist and to maintain their own way of life in a sort of religious underworld or subculture. For the modern state, whether it is democratic as in the United States, or communistic as in the U.S.S.R., or Fascist as in pre-war Italy and Germany, or nationalistic as in the new states of Asia and Africa, is no longer content to confine itself to certain limited functions like the liberal state of the nineteenth century. In fact all modern states are totalitarian in so far as they seek to embrace the spheres of economics and culture, as well as politics in the strict sense of the word. They are concerned not merely with the maintenance of public order and the defense of the people against its external enemies. They have taken on responsibility for all the different forms of communal activity which were formerly left to the individual or to independent social organizations such as the churches, and they watch over the welfare of their citizens from the cradle to the grave.

Thus the modern democratic state even in America is something quite different from the form of state envisaged by the men who formed the American Constitution. Generally speaking one can say that they were the enemies of state intervention and aimed at creating a system which would leave the community and the individual free to lead their own lives and frame their own cultural institutions. But the modern democratic state partakes of the nature of the Church. It is the educator and spiritual guide of its citizens and any influence which withdraws the citizen and especially the citizen's children from this universal guidance is felt to be undesirable, if not positively disloyal.

It is clear that such a situation is full of dangers for a Christian society. In the United States, at least, the danger is not acute at present. So long as an overwhelming majority of members of the American Congress are at least nominal church members, there is little possibility of the State adopting an actively anti-Christian policy. But the prospect for the future is more disquieting. For the more completely secularized public education becomes, and the more the State acquires an educational monopoly, as it is bound to do, considering the growing cost of education, the more the Christian element in our culture will diminish and the more complete will be the victory of secularization as the working religion, or rather counter-religion, of the American people. Even today the public school is widely regarded not as a purely educational institution in the nineteenth century sense—that is, as an elementary introduction to the literary and scientific traditions of culture—but as a moral training in citizenship, an initiation and indoctrination in the American way of life; and since the public school is essentially secular this means that only the secular aspects of American culture are recognized as valid. It is only a short step from here to the point at which the Christian way of life is condemned and outlawed as a deviation from the standard patterns of social behavior.

The Christians, like the Jews before them, have held that the fear of God is the beginning of wisdom, so that without the knowledge of God there can be no true education. Our modern secular civilization has decided otherwise. As the former head of UNESCO, Dr. Julian Huxley, has recently said, "Today God is becoming the erroneous hypothesis in all aspects of reality, including man's spiritual life."[3] Hence it seems clear that the present state of the post-Christian world, a world which is no longer Christian but which retains a vague sympathy for or sentimental attachment to Christian moral ideals, is essentially a temporary one. Unless there is a revival or restoration of Christian culture—of the social life

[3] *New Bottles for New Wine* (New York: Harper & Brothers, 1958), p. 272.

of the Christian community—modern civilization will become secularist in a more positive and aggressive way than it is today. And in a Godless civilization of this kind, it will be far more difficult for the individual Christian to exist and practice his religion than it has ever been before, even in ages of persecution. In the past, as for instance under the Roman Empire, the family formed an independent society which was almost immune from the state, so that it could become the primary cell of an unrecognized Christian society or culture. But today the very existence of the family as a social unit is threatened by the all-persuasive influence of the state and the secular mass culture. Yet without the Christian family there can be no Christian community life and indeed no church in the traditional sense of the word: only a few scattered individuals who maintain an isolated prophetic witness, like Elias in the wilderness.

But, it will be asked, is not the idea of a return to Christian civilization irreconcilable with the conditions of the modern world which are accepted today by Christians as well as secularists? Certainly there can be no question of a return to the old regime of the alliance of Church and State or the ecclesiastical domination of society. But this does not mean that we can afford to reject the ideal of a Christian civilization or the need for a return to spiritual unity. The kingdom of God is a universal kingdom: there is no aspect of human life that stands outside it or which is not in some way tributary to it. It is the nature of Christianity to be a world-transforming movement. It transforms humanity itself and in the course of this process it changes societies and civilizations. As St. Pius X wrote half a century ago, "To restore all things in Christ has always been the Church's motto, to restore in Christ not only what directly depends on the divine mission of the Church to lead souls to God but also, as we have explained, that which flows naturally from this divine mission, i.e.: Christian civilization in each and all the elements that compose it."

This same doctrine runs through the whole series of the social Encyclicals from the time of Leo XIII to the present time and I do not suppose that anyone will question that this is the normal accepted teaching of the Catholic Church. But, of course, it may be objected that this does not hold good for Protestants and that this is one of the main points on which Catholics and Protestants differ. This is certainly true of some Protestants and in our days the rejection of the idea of Christian civilization has become one of the hallmarks of the school of existentialist neo-Kierkegaardian Christianity which has had such an influence on the religious intelligentsia, if one may use the expression. But so far as my reading goes, it has never been characteristic of Protestantism in general. One of the most influential of the English Protestant thinkers of the last century, F. D. Maurice, made the positive affirmation of the universal kingship of Christ over every aspect of human culture and every form of human life the center of his whole teaching; and one of his modern disciples, Canon Alec Vidler, in his Hale lectures here in the United States some years ago, maintained that though Maurice may seem an isolated and almost fugitive thinker, his views are being endorsed by many of the most representative Biblical and dogmatic theologians of our day.

No doubt it is equally possible to find names on the opposite side; and in the United States especially there is an old established tradition of religious individualism and minority movements which is naturally uninterested in the problem of civilization in its religious aspects. This tradition, if I understand it right, is due to the meeting of two different influences —the Calvinist doctrine of the elect minority on the one hand, and the revivalist insistence on a particular type of intense religious experience on the other. But it certainly does not hold good of the Calvinist tradition in its pure form. For no Protestant was more insistent than Calvin on the importance of Christian standards in the life of the community and on the religious duties of the Christian State, and the same is true of the Puritans in New England. Indeed the reaction against the Puritans alike in seventeenth century England and in modern America was due to a resistance to the Puritan attempt to impose too rigid a standard of Calvinist ethics and culture on society. But here the attack came not from theologians who disbelieved in the possibility of a Christian civilization, but from humanists, or secularists who wished to emancipate culture from ecclesiastical control.

And the objections are still strong today. The average man's objection to Christian civilization is not an objection to medieval culture, which incorporated every act of social life in a sacred order of sacramental symbols and liturgical observances —such a culture is too remote from our experience to stir our emotions one way or the other: it is the dread of moral rigorism, of alcoholic prohibition or the censorship of books and films or of the fundamentalist banning of the teaching of biological evolution.

But what the advocates of a Christian civilization wish is not this narrowing of the cultural horizons, but just the reverse: the recovery of that spiritual dimension of social life the lack of which has cramped and darkened the culture of the modern world. We have acquired new resources of power and knowledge of which the old Christian civilization had hardly dreamed. Yet at the same time, we have lost that spiritual vision man formerly possessed—the sense of an eternal world on which the transitory temporal world of human affairs was dependent. This vision is not only a Christian insight: for it is intrinsic to the great civilizations of the ancient East and to the pagan world as well, so that it is not Christian civilization alone that is at stake. Here I think John Baillie, in his little book on *What is Christian Civilization?*, makes a useful and necessary distinction when he objects to the use of the word "pagan" to describe the dominant spirit of a secularist society.

> The word pagan [he says] is often unthinkingly used as if it meant a man who was devoid of all religious sentiment and worshipped no gods. But all real pagans are full of religious sentiment and their fundamental error rather lies in worshipping too many gods. The alternative today is not between being Christian or being pagan, but between being Christian and being nothing in particular, not between belonging to the Church and belonging to some social spiritual community that claims an equally wholehearted allegiance, but between belonging to the Church and belonging nowhere, giving no wholehearted allegiance to anything. Such is the tragedy that has overtaken so much of our common life that it belongs nowhere, has no spiritual home, no ultimate standards of reference and little definite conception of the direction in which it desires to move.[4]

I think this is surely true as a diagnosis of our present civilization. But society cannot remain stationary in this kind of spiritual no man's land. It will inevitably become a prey to the unclean spirits that seek to make their dwelling in the empty human soul. For a secular civilization that has no end beyond its own satisfaction is a monstrosity—a cancerous growth which will ultimately destroy itself. The only power that can liberate man from this kingdom of darkness is the Christian faith. For in the modern Western world there are no alternative solutions, no choice of possible other religions. It is a choice between Christianity or nothing. And Christianity is still a live option. The scattered elements of Christian tradition and Christian culture still exist in the modern world, though they may be

[4] John Baillie, *What is a Christian Civilization?* (New York: Oxford University Press, 1945), p. 39.

temporarily forgotten or neglected. Thus the revival of Christian civilization does not involve the creation of a totally new civilization, but rather the cultural reawakening or reactivization of the Christian minority. Our civilization has become secularized largely because the Christian element has adopted a passive attitude and allowed the leadership of culture to pass to the non-Christian minority. And this cultural passivity has not been due to any profound existentialist concern with the human predicament and divine judgment, but on the contrary to a tendency toward social conformity and too ready an acceptance of the values of a secularized society. It is the intellectual and social inertia of Christians that is the real obstacle to a restoration of Christian culture. For if it is true that more than half the population of this country are church members, Christians can hardly say that they are powerless to influence society. It is the will, not the power, that is lacking.

3
The Six Ages
of the Church

IN SPITE OF THE UNITY AND CONTINUITY OF the Christian tradition, each of the successive ages of the Church's history possesses its own distinctive character, and in each of them we can study a different facet of Christian life and culture. I reckon that there are six of these ages, each lasting for three or four centuries and each following a somewhat similar course. Each of them begin, and end, in crisis; and all of them, except perhaps the first, pass through three phases of growth and decay. First there is a period of intense spiritual activity when the Church is faced with a new historical situation and begins a new apostolate. Secondly there is a period of achievement when the Church seems to have conquered the world and is able to create a new Christian culture and new forms of life and art and thought. Thirdly there is a period of retreat when the Church is attacked by new enemies from within or without, and the achievements of the second phase are lost or depreciated.

At first sight these successive movements of achievement and retreat are a somewhat perplexing phenomenon since they seem to suggest that the history of Christianity is subject to some sociological law which limits its spiritual freedom and prevents the complete fulfillment of its universal mission. It is however a commonplace of Christian teaching that the life of the Church on earth is a continual warfare and that it cannot rely on any prospect of temporal and terrestrial success. From this point of view the successive ages of the Church are successive campaigns in this unending war, and as soon as one enemy has been conquered a new one appears to take its place.

This pattern of Christian history is found most clearly in *the First Age of the Church,* when from the first moment of its existence it became involved in a life-and-death struggle with the Roman Empire and with the civilization of the pagan world. And when after three centuries of conflict the Church was victorious and the Empire became Christian, the Church almost immediately had to face a new enemy in the form of a Christian heresy supported by the new Christian Empire. At the same time the first age of the Church is unique inasmuch as it was not following an existing tradition of faith and order as all the rest have done, but creating something absolutely new. Hence its initial phase, the Apostolic Age, stands in a sense outside the course of Church history as the archetype of spiritual creativity. For in that movement the creative activity of the Church was inseparable from the actual creation of the Church itself, so that Pentecost was at once the birthday of the Church and the beginning of the Church's apostolate. Moreover the new-born Church was faced almost at once with a second change of a more revolutionary character than she ever had to meet subsequently—that is to say, the extension of the apostolate from a Jewish to a Gentile environment and the incorporation in the new society of the great body of new converts drawn from the anonymous mass society of the great cosmopolitan centers of the Mediterranean world from Antioch to Rome itself. We have a contemporary account of this change in the New Testament and this gives us an invaluable and unique insight into the beginnings of the Church of the Gentiles. But we possess no comparable account of the change from the Judaeo-Christian point of view, nor are we much better informed with regard to the origins of the vernacular Syriac Christianity which was to have so great an importance for the future of the Church in the East.

But the main achievement of the first age of the Church was the successful penetration of the dominant urban Roman-Hellenistic culture and for this there is no lack of materials. Although the Church remained outside the pale of civic society, without legal rights and subjected to intermittent persecutions, it nevertheless became the greatest creative force in the culture of the Roman world in the second and third centuries. It created a new Christian literature, both Greek and Latin. It laid the foundations of a new Christian art, and above all, it created a new society which existed alongside of the established order of society and to some extent replaced it. There is perhaps no other example of a similar development of which we possess such a full historical record, and apart from its religious significance, it is also of great sociological interest, since the primitive Church was not a mere sectarian cult-organization but a real society with a strong sense of citizenship and a highly developed hierarchical order.

The cultural achievement of this first age reached its full development in the first half of the third century—the age of Clement and Origen in the East, of Tertullian and Cyprian in the West. But the third phase of cultural retreat and disintegration, which normally marks the later years of every age, hardly exists in this case; it was overshadowed by the vast catastrophe of the last great persecution which threatened to destroy the existence of the Church but actually ended in the Church's triumph.

The Second Age of the Church begins with the most spectacular of all the external victories which Christendom has known—the conversion of Constantine and the foundation of the new Christian capital of the Christian Empire. This marks the beginning of Christendom in the sense of a political society

D

or group of societies which find their principle of unity in the public profession of the Christian faith, and also of the Byzantine culture as the translation into Christian terms of the Hellenistic culture of the late Roman Empire. Both of them were to endure, for good or ill, for more than a thousand years, since the alliance of Church and State in a Christian Commonwealth which was inaugurated by Constantine and Theodosius remained a fundamental factor in Christian culture right down to the modern period.

But from the point of view of Church history, the three centuries or three hundred and thirty years between the Peace of the Church and the Moslem conquest of Jerusalem and Antioch and Alexandria have an internal unity and coherence. It has always been known as the Age of the Fathers *par excellence,* and both the Eastern and the Western Church have looked back to it as the classical age of Christian thought and the fountainhead of theological wisdom. The Fathers were not systematic theologians in the same sense as St. Thomas Aquinas and the great theologians of later periods. But they formed the mind of the Church and determined the norms of theological thought that were followed by the theologians of the Christian world in later centuries. In this way the three great Cappadocian Fathers, St. Basil, St. Gregory of Nazianzus and St. Gregory of Nyssa, remain the classical exponents of Eastern Orthodox theology, as St. John Chrysostom was the classical exponent of Scripture; while in the West St. Augustine was the seminal and creative mind that moulded the theological thought of the West, and St. Jerome laid the foundations of the Western tradition of Biblical and historical scholarship.

Now if we apply to this second age the threefold divisions which I described at the beginning of this chapter, we have first the period of creative achievement which covers the age of the greatest of the Fathers in East and West alike, from

St. Athanasius to St. Augustine, St. Jerome and St. John Chrysostom. This first century also saw the rise and development of Christian monasticism which had such an immense historical and spiritual influence on Christian culture and which represents the most distinctive contribution of the Oriental as opposed to the Hellenic element in Christianity. For though monasticism spread with extraordinary rapidity from one end of the Christian world to the other—from Persia and Mesopotamia to Gaul and the British Isles—it retained the imprint of its Egyptian origin. The solitary ascetics of the Nitrian desert and the cenobitical monasticism of St. Pachomius remained the two archetypes of the monastic life, whether in the center of the Byzantine world or in the barbarian societies of Wales and Ireland.

At the same time this first century also saw the flowering of Christian art and architecture and liturgical poetry, which reached their full development during the second phase of this period as the Eastern Empire became fully mature. The Age of Justinian was a great age of Christian culture in the sense that every aspect of social and artistic life was subject to Christian influence. St. Sophia and the basilicas of Ravenna still give us some idea of the greatness of Byzantine culture and the closeness of its association with the liturgy and with the life of the Church. Yet already the spiritual vitality of the age was beginning to flag and it was evident that the vast opportunity that had been offered to the Church of the previous period for the conversion of the Eastern world to Christianity had been lost.

During the last phase of the period the progressive alienation of the subject nationalities of the East from the state Church of the Byzantine Empire showed itself by the formation of new national churches that rejected the orthodox dogmas as formulated in the third and fourth general councils and were in open schism with Constantinople and Rome.

Finally the Age of the Fathers ended in the loss of the Christian East and the establishment of the new world power of Islam which separated not only Syria and Egypt but the rest of North Africa and the greater part of Spain from the community of Christian peoples. Thus at the beginning of *the Third Age* in the seventh century the Church found herself beset by enemies on all sides, by the Moslem aggression in the South and by the pagan barbarism of the North. In the South she failed to regain what had been lost, but she won the North by a long and painful missionary effort and thus laid the foundation of a new Christian culture which has been somewhat ineptly termed "medieval."

In this age, more than ever before or since, the Church was the sole representative of the higher culture and possessed a monopoly of all forms of literary education, so that the relation between religion and culture was closer than in any other period. The transplantation of Catholicism from the civilized Mediterranean world in which it had been born to the coasts of the Atlantic and the North Sea had far-reaching effects on its social organization. It ceased to be a predominantly urban religion; the old link between bishop and city was broken, and the monastery became the real center of life and Christian culture. There was a remarkable, but short-lived, flowering of Christian culture in these new lands which produced a classical historical record in the case of Bede's great *Ecclesiastical History of the English People*.

In the course of the eighth century this new Christian culture extended its influence to continental Europe by the work of the Irish and Anglo-Saxon missionaries, above all St. Boniface, who was the chief agent in bringing about the alliance of the Frankish monarchy, the Papacy and the Benedictine order which was the cornerstone not only of the Carolingian Empire but of the social order of Western Christendom in the Middle Ages. For the enduring importance of the Empire of Charles the Great is not to be found in its political achievements, which were ephemeral, but in its educational and liturgical work, which laid the foundations of that common Latin ecclesiastical culture which underlay the subsequent development of medieval civilization. On the other hand the attempt to create a new form of Christian state on these foundations, in the Anglo-Saxon kingdom and in the Carolingian Empire alike, failed owing to their lack of material resources and the absence of an educated class of lawyers and officials, such as still existed in the Byzantine world.

The collapse of the new Christian state under the pressure of the barbarian invasion was followed by a social relapse into a state of barbarism which threatened to overwhelm the Church itself. Nevertheless even in the darkest hour of this dark age the missionary apostolate of the Church continued, and the conversion of the Scandinavian peoples of the North and of the Czechs, the Poles and the Magyars, together with the Bulgarians and the Russians, in the East completed the task which had begun more than five centuries before, in the dark days of the barbarian invasions.

The *Fourth Age* of the Church began with a movement of spiritual reaction against the secularization of the Church and its absorption in the feudal society. It began as a movement of monastic reform in Lorraine and Burgundy and gradually extended its influence throughout Western Christendom. The turning point came in the middle of the eleventh century when the influence of the reformers reached Rome, and the Papacy put itself at the head of the movement to free the Church from its dependence on the feudal State and to restore the hierarchical order and the canonical discipline of Catholic tradition. Although this involved a tremendous and long-drawn-out conflict with the temporal power as represented by the Western Empire and the feudal principalities, it was not in principle a contest for political power. Its true aims are expressed in the final appeal which Gregory VII addressed to the Christian people from his exile in Salerno:

> Since the day when the Church placed me on its apostolic throne my whole desire and the end of all my striving has been that the Holy Church, the Bride of God, our mistress and our Mother, should recover her honor and remain free and chaste and Catholic.

So long as this alliance between the Papacy and the monastic reformers continued—that is to say, for nearly two and a half centuries—the Church exercised a dynamic influence on almost every aspect of Western culture; and the spiritual reformers, like St. Hugh of Cluny, St. Gregory VII, St. Anselm and above all St. Bernard, were also the central figures in the public life of Western Christendom. So too in the following period it was the influence of the Church that inspired the revival of Western learning and philosophy and the creation of the universities which were founded as international centers of higher study for Western Christendom as a whole.

Yet in spite of all this the movement of reform was never completely successful. The medieval Church was so deeply involved in the territorial economy of feudal society that it was not enough to free the Church from secular control so long as it retained its own temporal power and privileges. The reformers were indeed conscious of this dilemma and they found a personal solution in a strict adherence to the ascetic ideals of the monastic life, but this was not enough since even the most ascetic of the reformed orders, like the Cistercians, still remained wealthy and powerful in their corporate capacity. It was left to St. Francis, the Poor Man of Assisi, to take the further, final step by renouncing corporate property also and pledging his followers to total poverty. His ideal was not to found a new monastic order but to institute a new way of life, consisting in the simple and literal observance of the precepts of the Gospel, "the following of the poor life of Christ."

This marks the climax of the reforming movement, and the greatness of the medieval Papacy is nowhere more evident than in the way in which it accepted this drastic breach with the traditional order and made the new institution an organ for the evangelization of the masses and an instrument of its international mission. A century later this would not have been possible, for from the end of the thirteenth century the international unity of Western Christendom had begun to disintegrate and the alliance between Papacy and the party of religious reform was breaking down. During the last two centuries of the Fourth Age this disintegration shows itself in the defeat of the Papacy by the new national monarchies, like that of Philip IV of France, and in the rise of new revolutionary movements of reform, like the Wycliffites and the Hussites, and finally by the Great Schism in the Papacy itself. The attempt to overcome the schism by the Conciliar movement only widened the gap between the Northern European reformers and Rome, and the age ends with the acute secularization of the Renaisance Papacy and the great religious revolution of Northern Eurpoe which is known as the Reformation *par excellence*.

Thus *the Fifth Age of the Church* began in a time of crisis which threatened the unity and even the existence of Western Christendom. On the one hand there was the direct theological and ecclesiastical challenge of the Protestant Reformation which separated the greater part of Northern Europe from Catholicism, and on the other there was the cultural challenge of the new lay culture of the Italian Renaissance, which had replaced the theological and philosophical traditions of the medieval universities. Finally the external relations of Western Christendom had been transformed by the Turkish conquest of Southeastern Europe, and by the widening of the horizon of Western culture by the discovery of America and the opening of the Far East to European trade and navigation.

All these factors affected the character of Catholicism in the following age. The reaction against the Reformation produced the Tridentine reform of the Church and the revival of the religious life through the influence of new religious orders. The cultural issue was met by the development of a new form of Christian humanist culture and education, while the age of discovery was followed by a great outburst of missionary activity, which found its greatest representative in St. Francis Xavier, the apostle of the Far East. These new developments reached their maturity in the first half of the seventeenth century when the Catholic revival found expression in the new Baroque culture which dominated the artistic and intellectual life of Europe and represents the more or less successful fusion of the tradition of the humanist Renaissance and the spirit of the Catholic revival. In its religious aspect the most distinctive feature of this Baroque culture was the great development of Catholic mysticism which took place at this period and had a considerable influence on the art and literature of the age.

But the success of the Baroque culture was comparatively a short one. Its weakness, and that of the Catholic revival itself, was that it was too closely dependent on the success of the Catholic monarchies, especially the Hapsburg monarchies in Spain and Austria. When these declined, the Baroque culture declined with them, and when the third great Catholic monarchy was destroyed by the great political and social cataclysm of the French Revolution, the Church was the first victim of the change. As the armies of the French Republic advanced through Europe, the established order of the Catholic Church was swept away. The monasteries and universities were destroyed, church property was confiscated and the Pope himself was deported to France as a political prisoner. In the eyes of secular opinion, the Catholic Church had been abolished as a superannuated relic of the dead past.

Thus *the Sixth Age of the Church* began in an atmosphere of defeat and disaster. Everything had to be rebuilt from the foundations. The religious orders and the monasteries, the Catholic universities and colleges and, not least, the foreign missions had all been destroyed or reduced to poverty and impotence. Worst of all, the Church was still associated with the unpopular cause of the political reaction and the tradition of the *ancien régime*.

Yet in spite of all these disasters the Church did recover and a revival of Catholicism took place, so that the Church was in a far stronger position by 1850 than it had been a hundred years before when it still possessed its ancient wealth and privileges. This revival began in France during the Revolution, under the shadow of the guillotine, and the exiled French clergy contributed to the creation or restoration of Catholicism in England and America. Indeed the whole history of Catholicism in the United States belongs to this sixth age and is in many aspects typical of the new conditions of the period.

American Catholicism differs from that of the old world in that it is essentially urban, whereas in Europe it was still firmly rooted in the peasant population. Moreover from the beginning it has been entirely independent of the state and has not been restricted by the complex regime of concordats which was the dominant pattern of European Catholicism in the nineteenth century.

But at the present day it is the American rather than the European pattern which is becoming the normal condition of the Church everywhere except in those regions like Eastern Europe or China where it exists on sufferance or under persecution. I will say no more about the present age as it is dangerous to generalize about a period which is still unfinished. The present age of the Church still has centuries to run and who can say what even the present century will bring forth? On the one hand Christians are faced with an external threat more formidable than anything we have known since the time of Islam. On the other hand the intellectual and spiritual lassitude that marked the last two centuries has largely disappeared and we see on every side the awakening of a new apostolic spirit and a wider concern for the unity of the Church.

Each of these ages has only a limited duration; each ends in a crisis, a divine judgment in which a whole social world is destroyed. And insofar as these social worlds have been Christian ones, their downfall creates a problem for the Christian who sees so much that appeared to be part of the consecrated, God-given order swept away together with the evils and abuses of a corrupt society. This however is only a particular example of the problem of the relativity of culture with which all historians have to deal. But whereas the secular historian is in no way committed to the cultures of the past, the Catholic, and indeed every Christian, is bound to recognize the existence of a transcendent supra-temporal element at work in history. The Church exists in history, but it transcends history so that each of its temporal manifestations has a supernatural value and significance. To the Catholic all the successive ages of the Church and all the forms of Christian culture form part of one living whole in which we still participate as a contemporary reality.

One of the main reasons why I dissent from the current threefold division or periodization of Church history as ancient, medieval and modern is that it is apt to make us lose sight of the multiplicity and variety of the life of the Church, and of the inexhaustible fecundity with which, in the words of the liturgy of Easter Day, God continually calls new peoples into the divine society, multiplying the Church by the vocation of the Gentiles. I have spoken of the Six Ages of the Church— there may be sixty before the universal mission of the Church is completed. But each age has its own peculiar vocation which can never be replaced, and each, to paraphrase Ranke's famous saying, stands in a direct relation to God and answers to Him alone for its achievements and its failures. Each too bears its own irreplaceable witness to the faith of all.

4
Christian Culture as a Culture of Hope

THE SCIENCE OF CULTURE—CULTURE HISTORY, cultural morphology and the comparative study of cultures— is of very recent origin. It grew up in the nineteenth century with the development of the new social sciences, above all anthropology, and it had no place in the traditional curriculum of liberal education. But during the present century its development has been rapid, especially perhaps in Germany and in America, so that today it is no longer confined to scientific specialists but has been adopted, however superficially, by publicists and politicians and has a growing influence on modern social thought.

Nevertheless there still remains a certain contradiction and confusion between this new idea of culture and the old unitary conception which is deeply rooted in our educational traditions. To the average educated man culture is still regarded as an absolute. Civilization is one: men may be more cultured or less cultured, but in so far as they are cultured, they are all walking along the same high road which leads to the same goal. The idea that there are a number of different roads leading, perhaps, in opposite directions, still remains a difficult idea to assimilate. Humanism, the Enlightenment and the modern conceptions of "the democratic way of life" and the "one world" all presuppose the same idea of a single universal ideal of civilization toward which all men and peoples must move.

Against this we have the anthropologist's and ethnologist's conception of a culture as an artificial creation which has been constructed by particular men in particular circumstances for particular ends. The cultures are as diverse as races and languages and states. A culture is built, like a state, by the labor of generations which elaborate a way of life suited to their needs and environment and consequently different from the way of life of other men in other circumstances. The Negro in the tropical rain forest makes his own terms with life which are different from those of the herdsman of the steppes, as these terms again are different from the ways of the hunters of the Arctic. All these simple cultures have their limits set by nature. They cannot go far, but they can endure indefinitely, until their environment is changed or some external force, like a conquering race, displaces or destroys them. The primitive existence of the Eskimos or the Bushmen is in a sense timeless and has remained outside history, so that it seems to take us back to a prehistoric world.

But with the higher cultures this is not so. They are essentially the children of time and of history, and the more they emancipate themselves from their primitive dependence on nature, the more closely do they become confined to the human restrictions and laws of the artificial social world that they create. We see this tendency already operating in barbarian cultures like those of Polynesia where social institutions are fortified and protected by an elaborate system of taboos which seem so inexplicable and irrational to the foreign observer. And yet the same principle is to be found in the more advanced cultures. In fact the more advanced they are, the more elaborate are the artificial rules of caste and status, of custom and law, of ceremonial and etiquette with which they surround themselves. It is the great paradox of civilization that every victory over nature, every increase of social control, also increases the burden of humanity. When man builds a fortress he also builds a prison, and the stronger it is, the greater its cost in human suffering.

When we look back at the civilizations of the past, we cannot fail to be impressed by their achievements. The Egyptian pyramids still stand today after nearly five thousand years as monuments of human power. But while we marvel we are appalled at the suffering and the waste of human labor that they represent. For at the heart of the pyramid there is nothing but the corpse of a despot.

So too in Mesopotamia, it was from the spectacle of those vast artificial mountains or ziggurats which towered over the cities of Babylonia that the inspired writer drew his image of the nemesis of human power and pride—the curse of Babel. For whenever a culture reaches its culmination of power and social control, as in the age of the pyramids or the Empires of Babylon and Rome, it breaks down under its own weight which has become too heavy for human nature to endure, and so the whole process has to begin again until a new Babylon has been built.

Now it may be said that this is true of the slave states and military empires of the past but that humanity has freed itself from this curse by the scientific control of nature and that democracy and socialism open the prospect of universal happiness to the oppressed and exploited who have hitherto carried the burden of civilization without receiving its benefits. St. Just said, "Happiness is a new idea in Europe," and for a century and a half Western culture has been sustained by this hope of the immediate coming of a social millennium. But during the last forty years the old devils which seemed to have been banished have returned with sevenfold force, so that at the present moment civilization is suffering from a sense of pessimism and frustration and loss of hope which finds poignant expression in such works as George Orwell's *1984*. It is not merely that the socialist paradise has turned into the totalitarian hell; even worse is the deception of scientific progress which promised the nineteenth century a new world and has given the twentieth century the atomic bomb.

There are some Christians who feel a certain satisfaction—a kind of *Schadenfreude*—at the sudden collapse of the liberal idealism of the nineteenth century and the loss of hope in the future of modern civilization. Christianity, they say, is a religion of crisis, a judgment which regards even the highest achievements of human culture as vitiated by man's fallen nature and doomed to destruction. This no doubt is the tradition of the Calvinist and the Jansenist and it finds a certain justification in the history of the past with its record of the frustration of achievement and the death of cultures. Nevertheless this is essentially a one-sided view. Christianity is certainly not to be identified with religious individualism or with the rejection of history and the condemnation of culture.

On the contrary there is no religion, and perhaps no philosophy, which is so deeply concerned with man as part of a community or which attaches a higher significance to history. For Christianity is essentially the religion of the Incarnation, of the divine intervention in history at a particular time and in a particular social context and of the extension and incorporation of this new spiritual creation in the life of humanity through the mediation of an historic institutional society.

Hence while Christianity rejects the modern optimistic illusion of an automatic process of material progress which leads inevitably to a social millennium, it does not deny the existence of progress in a deeper sense. On the contrary it teaches that throughout the ages the life of humanity is being leavened and permeated by a transcendent principle, and every culture or human way of life is capable of being influenced and remoulded by this divine influence. Thus Christianity has always been a culturally creative force. It came first into a world which was overcivilized, where the social soil was becoming exhausted and the burden of empire and law was becoming too heavy for human nature to bear. And it transformed and renewed this civilization, not by any program of social or political reform but by revealing the existence of a new spiritual dimension and bringing the light of hope to those who sat in darkness and in the shadow of death.

An English writer of the last century has described in a remarkable passage how this atmosphere of hope pervades the art of the catacombs and the cult of the martyrs with the promise of the dawn of a new Christian culture.

> Penetrating the whole atmosphere, touching everything around with its peculiar sentiment, it seemed to make all this visible mortality, death itself, more beautiful than any fantastic dream of old mythology had hoped to make it; and that in a simple sincerity of feeling about a supposed actual fact. The thought, the word, *Pax—Pax Tecum!*—was put forth everywhere, with images of hope, snatched sometimes even from that jaded pagan world, which had really afforded men so little of it, from first to last, of succour, of regeneration, of escape from death—Hercules wrestling with Death for possession of Alcestis, Orpheus taming the wild beasts, the Shepherd with his sheep, the Shepherd carrying the sick lamb upon his shoulders. Only, after all, these imageries formed but the slightest contribution to the whole dominant effect of tranquil hope, there— of a kind of heroic cheerfulness and grateful expansion of the heart; again, as with the sense of some real deliverance; and which seemed actually to deepen, the longer one lingered through these strange and fearful passages. A figure, partly pagan, yet the most frequently repeated of all these visible parables—the figure of one

just escaped as if from the sea, still in strengthless, sur-
prised joy, clinging to the very verge of the shore—together with the inscription beneath it, seemed best to
express the sentiment of the whole.

> I went down to the bottom of the mountains;
> The earth with her bars was about me forever;
> Yet hast Thou brought up my life from corruption.[1]

The remaking of an old culture by the birth of a new hope
was not the conscious aim of the Christians themselves. They
tended, like St. Cyprian, to believe that the world was growing
old, that the empire was irremediably pagan and that some
world catastrophe was imminent. Nevertheless they lived in a
spiritual atmosphere of hope, and this atmosphere gradually
spread until the climate of the world was changed. The heart-
less, hopeless Rome which found its monstrous expression in
the Colosseum and the gladiatorial games became the Rome
of St. Leo and St. Gregory—a city which laid the foundations
of a new world while its own world was falling in ruin around
it.

We see the same process at work in northern Europe during
the Dark Ages. The men who converted the warrior peoples
of the North and laid the foundations of medieval culture had
no conception of the new world that they were creating and
no belief in the temporal future of civilization. But they were
men of hope, as they were men of faith, and therefore their
work endured for a thousand years and bore rich fruit in every
field of cultural activity, as well as on its own religious level.

This is the paradox of Christendom which so impressed
G. K. Chesterton and which is the theme of his longest poem,
The Ballad of the White Horse. It is the paradox that the
pagan worship of nature is in the end a religion of death,

[1] Walter Pater, *Marius the Epicurean*, 1885, II, pp. 117–18 (first
edition).

E

while the Christian who is indifferent to the temporal results of his actions is the servant and guardian of life.

Chesterton's Christian optimism is out of fashion today, when the external perils of Western civilization are reflected in the moral discouragement and spiritual anxiety of Western man. Nor is this confined to the non-Christian world. It is impossible to deny that there have been tendencies in Western Christianity which are actually inimical to that spirit of hope which inspired the Christian culture of the past.

At the moment when the Renaissance announced a new faith in man and a new hope in the possibilities of human culture, the Reformers reacted in the opposite direction by the pessimism of their views on the total corruption of human nature and the rigorism of their doctrines of predestination and election. Nor was this tendency confined to the Protestant world; it was also present in the Catholic world in the form of Jansenism, and though Jansenism was always a minority movement it would be difficult to exaggerate the extent to which it divided the Christian mind and depressed the Christian spirit. No doubt neither Calvin nor Saint-Cyran consciously denied the traditional Christian hope. But it is no less certain that the practical effect of their teaching was to erect a barrier between religion and life which contributed so largely to the progressive secularization of Western culture. Thus we see in the classical culture of the *grand siècle* how this Jansenist rigorism combined with the Renaissance prejudice against the "gothic" barbarism of medieval culture to make Boileau ban the traditional religious drama of the Christian past—a tradition which was still flourishing in Spain when Boileau wrote:

> De la Foy des Chrestiens les Mystères terribles
> D'ornaments Egayez ne sont pas susceptibles.
> L'Évangile à l'Esprit n'offre de tous costez,
> Que pénitence à faire, et tourmens méritez.

> The mysteries which Christians must believe
> Disdain such shifting pageants to receive.
> The Gospel offers nothing to our thoughts
> But penitence, or punishment for faults.

In Protestant Europe it was not only the religious drama that was outlawed but Christian art as well, and with it disappeared all the other expressions of Christian culture which united the Church with the life of the people. Religion became a specialized activity which was confined to church and chapel and limited to one day in the week. Thus the destruction of Christian culture was the work of the Christians themselves who allowed the new Babylon of modern materialist civilization to be built on the soil of Christendom.

But this failure or abdication on the part of Christians in the past is no reason for despair in the present. The loss of hope was indeed the source from which all these ills have flowed, for when men were deprived of spiritual hope, it was inevitable that they should turn eagerly to the new secular hope of a social millennium held out to them by the preachers of materialism.

But today, as we have seen, these hopes have proved delusive and the new Babylon is threatened by an even more catastrophic and suicidal end than any of the world empires of the past. Thus we find ourselves back in the same situation as that which the Christians encountered during the decline of the ancient world. Everything depends on whether the Christians of the new age are equal to their mission—whether they are able to communicate their hope to a world in which man finds himself alone and helpless before the monstrous forces which have been created by man to serve his own ends but which have now escaped from his control and threaten to destroy him.

5

The Institutional Forms
of Christian Culture

WE CANNOT SEPARATE CULTURE FROM RELI-
gion any more than we can separate our life from our faith.
As a living faith must change the life of the believer, so a living religion must influence and transform the social way of
life—that is to say, the culture. It is impossible to be a Christian
in church and a secularist or a pagan outside. Even a Christian
minority, which lives a hidden and persecuted life, like the
early Christians in the ages of the catacombs, possesses its own
patterns of life and thought, which are the seeds of a new
culture.

Nevertheless it must be admitted that Christians are some-
times opposed to the very idea of Christian culture, since it
seems to lead to an identification between a religious reality
which is absolute and divine and a social reality which is limited and human. It was this point which inspired Kierkegaard's
tremendous onslaught on "Christendom" as a colossal fraud—
a betrayal of Christianity. He writes:

> What we have before us is not Christianity but a
> prodigious illusion, and the people are not pagans but
> live in the blissful conceit that they are Christians.[1]
> When one sees what it is to be a Christian in Den-

[1] S. Kierkegaard, *Attack upon "Christendom,"* trans. by Walter Low-
rie (Princeton: Princeton University Press, 1944), p. 97.

mark, how could it occur to anyone that this is what Jesus Christ talks about: cross and agony and suffering, crucifying the flesh, suffering for the doctrine, being salt, being sacrificed, etc.? No, in Protestantism, especially in Denmark, Christianity marches to a different melody, to the tune of "Merrily we roll along, roll along, roll along!"—Christianity is enjoyment of life, tranquillized, as neither the Jew nor the pagan was, by the assurance that the thing about eternity is settled, settled precisely in order that we might find pleasure in enjoying this life, as well as any pagan or Jew.[2]

God's thought in introducing Christianity was, if I may venture to say so, to pound the table hard in front of us men. . . . God succeeded in this, he really overawed men. But gradually the human race came to itself, and shrewd as it is, it saw that to do away with Christianity by force was not practicable—"so let us do it by cunning," they said. We are all Christians and so Christianity is *eo ipso* abolished.[3]

Man's knavish interest consists in creating millions and millions of Christians, the more the better, all men if possible; for thus the whole difficulty of being a Christian vanishes, being a Christian and being a man amounts to the same thing, and we find ourselves where paganism ended.

Christendom has mocked God and continues to mock Him—just as if to a man who is a lover of nuts, instead of bringing him one nut with a kernel, we were to bring him tons and millions of empty nut-shells.[4]

What Kierkegaard attacked with such passion, however, was not Christendom but the secularization of Christendom, and especially that particular form of secularization which he found in the Danish State Church of the mid-nineteenth cen-

2 *Ibid.,* pp. 34–35.
3 *Ibid.,* pp. 166–67.
4 *Ibid.,* p. 156.

tury. For he was living in a culture which was undergoing a rapid and complete process of secularization, and what infuriated him was the refusal of the clergy to admit the real state of affairs, so long as they could retain their official status and prerogatives.

But the fact that Christian culture had become moribund in Denmark in 1850 does not prove that it had never existed. There had been a time, as he himself admitted, when "Christendom" had meant something. Christianity was a historical reality which had actually come into the world and had transformed the societies with which it came into contact. Leaving aside for the moment the question of the relation between the religious ideal of Christianity and the social forms in which it embodied itself, there can be no doubt that Christianity in the past has been a creative cultural force of the first magnitude, and that it has actually created a Christian culture or a number of Christian cultures. The same, of course, is true of other religions. In fact every great civilization that exists in the world today has a great religious tradition associated with it, and it is impossible to understand the culture unless we understand the religion that lies behind it.

This is accepted by the orientalist and usually also by the student of more primitive cultures. No one pretends to understand Arab or Persian culture without knowing something about Islam and the beliefs and institutions that are common to the whole Moslem world. Only in the case of Europe has this elementary consideration been neglected. We have had countless studies of Western culture and histories of European society which leave out Christianity or treat it as of secondary importance.

To a great extent this state of things is due to that educational schism of which I have spoken elsewhere. Our approach to the study of our culture has been influenced for centuries by the image of an idealized classical culture which was treated as the absolute standard of Western culture, so that whatever conflicted with or diverged from this was ignored as barbarous.

But this is not the only factor. For in addition to the cultural idealism of the humanists there was also a religious idealism which had a very similar effect on men's judgments on the history of Western culture. For at the time that the humanists were exalting the ideal of a classical culture which had been forgotten for a thousand years, the reformers were preaching the return to an ideal type of Christianity which had also been lost for a thousand years.

The cumulative effect of these tendencies was to turn men's attention away from the historical reality of Christian culture and toward an ideal classical culture and an ideal primitive Christianity, so that in looking for something that was not there, they overlooked the things that were before their eyes— the historical forms of Western Christian culture as they had actually existed.

But by this time these historical forms have become remote and unfamiliar, so that it is necessary to study them anew in the same objective way in which we study the great oriental cultures of the past. Indeed in many respects the Christian culture of the past resembles the culture of Islam more than it resembles modern Western culture. Nor is this surprising, since the three great Western religions—Judaism, Christianity and Islam—are closely related to one another and share a number of common features. In all of them, in contrast to the modern world, the primary social bond was not political but religious, and consequently a man's relation to his religious community had many of the characteristics that we associate with political citizenship. The religious community was the absolute one, and all other communities—family, state and nation—were relative ones, parts of a greater whole.

In the second place all these cultures centered in a tradition of sacred learning: a divine Scripture, a sacred law, a sacred history and a sacred oral tradition. This sacred tradition was alone regarded as learning in the absolute sense. In some cases this sacred learning might represent the whole of learning and the only literary culture; in other cases there was also a tradition of secular learning, but this was secondary and supplementary.

In the third place in all these cultures the first social duty, and consequently the primary cultural activity, was the act of worship. In Islam this act was so closely connected with the recitation of the Koran that it produced little liturgical development, yet even so it holds a central place in Moslem culture.

In Christianity, on the other hand, the liturgy was the center of a rich tradition of religious poetry and music and artistic symbolism. In fact the art of Christendom in both its Byzantine and medieval phases was essentially a liturgical art which cannot be understood without some knowledge of the liturgy itself and its historical origin and development. And the same is true to a great extent of popular and vernacular culture. The popular religious drama, which had such an important influence on the rise of European drama as a whole, was either a liturgical drama in the strict sense, like the Passion plays and Nativity plays, or was directly related to the cult of the saints and the celebration of their feasts. For the cult of the saints, which had its basis in the liturgy, was the source of a vast popular mythology and provided a bridge between the higher ecclesiastical and literary culture and the peasant culture with its archaic traditions of folklore and magic.

In the same way the church itself—I mean the liturgical edifice—was at the same time the organ of both the higher and the lower culture, and consequently a great instrument of social integration. On the one hand it was the temple in which the liturgy was celebrated in the common language of educated Christendom, and, on the other, in the village and the pilgrimage place it was the center of the common people for whom it was at once school and theater and picture gallery.

It is at this point that the cultural division produced by the Reformation is seen most clearly. The church ceased to be the organ of popular culture in art and symbolism. It retained its educational importance to a great extent, but the change of the liturgy changed the nature of the religious culture. And thus while in Catholic Europe, as for example in Spain, the drama and painting and sculpture retained their religious character and were still the organs of a Christian culture common to the educated and the uneducated, in Protestant Europe the arts became secularized and the Bible only—the reading of the Bible and the preaching of the Bible—became the chief and almost the only vehicle of Christian culture.

In all these respects there is a remarkable agreement between the cultures of Byzantine Orthodoxy and Western Catholicism. The liturgies are different, the art is different, the music is different, but there is the same organic relation between them in the two cultures. The Byzantine attitude to the Holy Images is more rigid and in a sense more theological than the Western attitude to the images of the saints, but there is the same conception of religious art as a necessary organ of Christian culture and there is the same attitude to the cult of the saints as the mirrors of Christian perfection and the mediators between the spiritual and sensible worlds. Moreover both cultures share the same conception of spiritual hierarchy—that analogy between the ecclesiastical and the celestial hierarchies which is one of the keys to the traditional Christian conception of the universal order.

Finally there is one great religious institution which is common to the two cultures and which has perhaps had a greater and more direct influence on the formation of Christian culture than any other single factor: I mean the Monastic Order. It is in monasticism that religion and culture attain their most complete fusion. For the monastic rule is a sacred law which is applied to every detail of individual life and becomes the basis of a common way of life and a common society. So the latter was in principle a totally Christian society in which there was no longer any room for the conflict between religious and secular standards, a society without private property or family bonds or political and military obligations. At first sight it seems an impossible system, since its social order rests on the denial of the three main forces which have created society— sex and war and economic acquisitiveness. Nevertheless, in spite of manifold failures, it exerted a dynamic influence on every aspect of Christian culture. Its influence on the new Christian society of the barbarian North, where there was no tradition of city culture, was especially important. Here the coming of the monks meant not only a new religious way of life but a new civilization, so that the Western monasteries were islands of Christian culture in a sea of barbarism.

No institution in the history of Christian culture has been more intensively studied than this. But the best studies are those of particular orders and monasteries, and I do not think there is any work which deals adequately with Christian monasticism as a whole and particularly with the relation between the different forms of monasticism and the different forms of Christian culture. We can distinguish a number of successive types of monasticism, each of which is typical of a particular phase in the development of Christian culture.

First there is the original oriental type of monasticism, as it was organized by St. Pachomius in Egypt in the year 323, and which was rapidly diffused from one end of the Christian world to the other. This is the form of monasticism which was practically the creator of Celtic Christian culture and determined the ecclesiastical character of the Celtic Church.

Second there is Benedictine monasticism, which is the classical type of Western monasticism and was the foundation of

Carolingian and early medieval culture and of Western education. From this common Benedictine tradition there developed first the Cluniac reform of the tenth century, and second the Cistercian order, which attained such a vast extension in the twelfth century and which was the first religious order in the modern sense of the word.

Third there are the Friars, above all the Franciscans and the Dominicans, who were the leading force in thirteenth-century culture and who played such a decisive part in the life of the medieval universities and in the development of scholastic philosophy.

Finally there are the Jesuits, the great Counter Reformation order, whose influence on the post-Renaissance and Baroque culture of Catholic Europe can hardly be exaggerated, above all in the sphere of education.

Thus the development of monasticism corresponds very closely with the development of Christian culture, so that the history of Christian culture is comprised in the one thousand four hundred and fifty years between the foundation of the first monastery by St. Pachomius at Tabennisi in 323 to the dissolution of the Society of Jesus in 1773.

Of course this criterion excludes the culture of Protestant Europe, and in fact it was the dissolution of the monasteries and the rejection of the monastic ideal which, more than any theological question or any question of ecclesiastical order, was the revolutionary change that separated Protestant Europe from the Christian culture of the past. Nevertheless, the same spiritual forces which produced monasticism remained active in the Protestant world.

This activity is to be seen in the formation of the sects, considered not as theological doctrines but as new ways of religious life. And accordingly, if we wish to find the sociological analogies of the religious orders in the Protestant world we must look to such organizations as the Anabaptists, the

Puritan sects, the Pietists, the Quakers, the Methodists and the Plymouth Brothers (not to mention the more eccentric American developments, like the Shakers, which went so far as to insist on celibacy and the community of property).

In some of these sects, like the Dunkers and the Amana Society, we find a conscious attempt to create a totally separate Christian culture with its own economic and social order, its own forms of dress and behavior and even its own rudimentary forms of art. But none of them have any historical or religious importance except as specimens of eccentric development.

Excluding these extreme and abnormal types, this sectarian development has had considerable influence on the culture of Protestant Europe and America, as has been shown in detail by writers like Max Weber and Ernst Troeltsch. But in so far as sectarianism involves the separation of church and state and regards secular society as a neutral field common to the different sectarian groups, each of which is spiritually self-contained, it has been a factor which has made for the secularization of culture, or for that semi-secularized type of culture that was characteristic of Britain and the United States of America in the nineteenth century.

Nevertheless, as we cannot understand Western culture as a whole without a study of the great Christian culture which lies behind it, so also we cannot understand the culture of modern England and Wales and America unless we have studied the underworld of sectarian Christianity—a world which has been so neglected by the political and economic historian, but which none the less contributed so many vital elements to the complex pattern of nineteenth-century society.

This, however, is a digression; what I am primarily concerned with is the need for a more thorough and systematic study of the main tradition of Christian culture in its three great phases: the Age of the Fathers, the Middle Ages, and the Baroque period. For it is only by this large-scale study of a whole civilization, covering many centuries of continuous development, that we can understand the process of change by which a new religion enters an old society and is partially assimilated by it, so that the way of life of the society as well as of the individual is changed; and how out of this process a new culture arises which may be transmitted to other societies and may change them also.

Furthermore it is essential for us to study this particular religion-culture because it is the source of our own culture; and our judgment of other religions and other cultures must inevitably be seen through this medium. For the idea that the historian or the sociologist is in a privileged position, from which he can study any and every culture and religion in Olympian detachment, is really an absurdity and the source of countless errors and absurdities in thought and practice.

Finally there is a peculiar value in the study of Christian culture, because there is no culture that illustrates so completely the essential dualism of religion and culture and the element of conflict and spiritual tension which this dualism involves. There are societies, especially the more primitive and backward societies, in which this dualism seems absent, and in these cases religion becomes inseparable from custom and has little or no dynamic importance as a cause of social change. On the other hand there are religions that are nonsocial, which expressly disassociate themselves from any responsibility for social life and culture, and while these often possess considerable dynamic energy their appeal is a negative one, so that they are revolutionary and subversive forces.

But in Christianity the tendency to a world-renouncing asceticism coexists with a tendency toward social and cultural activity, and it is the tension of these two forces that has given Christianity its characteristic power to change society and to create new cultural forms.

This question of the influence of Christianity on social

change has received a good deal more attention from the historians recently than it did in the past. In particular, a number of writers like Stepun and Berdyaev have interpreted the Russian revolutionary movement in terms of the Russian religious traditions—both the tradition of the Orthodox Church and that of the sects. So too, in the case of English history, the late Elie Halévy attributed great importance to the rise of Methodism and the Evangelical Movement in the eighteenth and nineteenth centuries, but for the opposite reason—that is, as one of the main causes of the nonrevolutionary character of the development of English society in the age of the French Revolution.

In all these ways the study of Christian culture is important to the historian. But above all, far outweighing any other consideration, there is the fact that Christian culture was identical with Western culture during the centuries of formation and growth, and that it was the integrative force which first united the different peoples of Western Europe in a new community. What Hellenism was to the ancient world, Christendom has been to the modern. So that to attempt to understand the modern world without any study of Christian culture is as difficult as it would be to understand the Roman world without any knowledge of Hellenism.

6
Civilization in Crisis

WE HAVE BECOME ACCUSTOMED TO TAKING
the secular character of modern civilization for granted. We
have most of us never known anything else and consequently
we are apt to think that this is a natural and normal state of
things, so that whatever our own beliefs may be, we do not
expect modern civilization to pay much attention to religion,
still less to be based upon a religious conception of existence.

Actually, of course, this state of things is far from being
normal; on the contrary, it is unusual and perhaps unique. If
we look back and out over the world and across the centuries,
we shall see how exceptional and abnormal it is. It is hardly
too much to say that all civilizations have always been religious
—and not only civilizations but barbarian and primitive societies also. For in the past man's social life has never been
regarded as something that existed in its own right as a law
to itself. It was seen as dependent on another more permanent
world, so that all human institutions were firmly anchored by
faith and law to the realities of this higher world. No doubt
human life in the past was more insecure than it is today,
more precarious and more exposed to violence and to the catastrophic accidents of famine and pestilence. But on the other
hand this world of disorder and suffering was only a part of
reality. It was balanced and compensated by the larger, more
permanent world from which man came and to which he returned. So that a civilization was not just a highly organized

form of social existence with its industry and art and scientific technique, it was both social and religious—two worlds of reality bound together by a visible fabric of institutions and laws, and by objective conceptions of justice and authority which gave them validity.

As I have shown in *Religion and Culture* and elsewhere, all the great civilizations of the ancient world believed in a transcendent divine order which manifested itself alike in the cosmic order—the law of heaven; in the moral order—the law of justice; and in religious ritual; and it was only in so far as society was co-ordinated with the divine order by the sacred religious order of ritual and sacrifice that it had the right to exist and to be considered a civilized way of life.

But today this ancient wisdom is forgotten. Civilization has cut adrift from its old moorings and is floating on a tide of change. Custom and tradition and law and authority have lost their old sacredness and moral prestige. They have all become the servants of public opinion and of the will of society. They have become humanized and secularized and at the same time unstable and fluid. As civilization becomes materially richer and more powerful, it becomes spiritually or religiously weaker and poorer. For a long time in Europe in the eighteenth and nineteenth centuries and to some extent in America today, this state of things was welcomed as a positive achievement. Individual freedom, political democracy and economic progress were regarded as ends in themselves, which would provide their own solutions to the problems that they created. It was believed that the secularization of culture was favorable to human freedom, since men would be freed from the incubus of authority in Church and State, and the functions of the latter would be reduced to that of a neutral guardian of order and security. In fact, however, the progress of scientific technique has led to the increasing concentration of power. Even the weakest and the mildest of modern governments possesses a universal power of control over the lives of its citizens which the absolute monarchies of the past never dreamt of.

Nevertheless this enormous concentration of power, which is to be seen alike in politics and economics and scientific technique, does not produce moral prestige as in the past. The politician and the civil servant do not possess the *mana* of the barbarian chief or the sacred majesty of ancient kingship, and it is the same with the industrialist and the scientific technologist. They are all regarded as ordinary men who have happened to succeed in their professions and have climbed to the top of the tree.

But it is questionable whether this state of things can last, for there is a glaring disproportion between the terrifying reality of power and the fragility and unimportance of the men who control it. And in fact during the last generation we have seen a violent reaction against the liberal ideology of the nineteenth century. First in Russia and then in Western Europe and in Eastern Asia, we have seen a series of attempts to unite the new forces of technology and scientific control with political absolutism and ideological orthodoxy. In this new totalitarian order individual freedom has been sacrificed, criticism has been outlawed, and science and technology have been forced to serve the will of authority and to justify the doctrines of the dominant ideology.

How does this affect the problem of secularization? Obviously its immediate direct effect is to cause an intensification of the process, since it makes it practically impossible for religious minorities to preserve their cultural autonomy or even to exist. The official ideology of the totalitarian state is itself completely secular and it is imposed compulsorily on the whole society, not only by party propaganda but by the convergent pressure of government action in every field of cultural and educational activity.

But indirectly and in the long run, all this may have a very

F

different effect from that which was originally envisaged by
the politicians. For when a revolutionary ideology is transformed from a minority protest into an official orthodoxy, it
changes its nature and acquires many of the psychological
characteristics of a religion.

Seen from this point of view its real *raison d'être* is not to
carry on the process of secularization but to provide a substitute for religion, to stop modern civilization from drifting
aimlessly and to anchor it again securely to absolute immutable
principles which are beyond the reach of criticism.

It is difficult for us in the West to consider this aspect of
totalitarianism dispassionately, since as Christians our objection to totalitarianism as a counter-religion is even greater than
our objection as Westerners to the totalitarian suppression of
individual liberty and the right of criticism. Nevertheless the
sweeping victories of Communism in Asia and the growing
unpopularity there of the Western democratic ideology make
it a matter of life and death to understand the real nature of
the totalitarian appeal, whether we call it religious or antireligious.

We must face the fact that Western political ideals—democracy, liberty, equality and the like—are the product of a particular cultural tradition and represent the experience and
achievement of certain privileged peoples and classes—the
citizen class in ancient Greece, the free estates of medieval
Christendom, and the bourgeoisie and free churches of modern
Europe and America. The greater part of the world has never
known these things. In Asia and Africa life has been short
and hard and uncertain. Constitutional government and individual political rights have been unknown and there has
been no appeal or legal protection from the decrees of arbitrary
power. The only alternative has been between a paternal despotism which protects the peasant in his life and his labor and

a ruthless exploitation which leaves him at the mercy of the tax gatherer and the money-lender.

In such a world the evils of totalitarianism which shock the Western mind—its denial of personal liberty, of freedom of opinion and free enterprise—are less apparent than the evils of misgovernment and the oppression of class by class which it professes to cure. From the Oriental standpoint Communism represents the return to a familiar pattern—the traditional order of authoritarianism and mass responsibility. It demands everything—absolute loyalty, absolute obedience to the state and the utter subordination of the individual to the community; but in return it makes men feel that there is a power watching over them which is immune from human weakness and is based on an unchanging foundation of absolute principles.

A faith of this kind is a religion in the subjective sense—a way of salvation for man, though it is not religion in the objective theological sense.

But, it may be asked, if Communism is viewed in this light, why should it prove so attractive to Asians who are already well provided with real theological religions? The answer, I think, is that the great Oriental religions are no longer culturally active and that they have become divorced from social life and from contemporary culture. This explanation is borne out by a remarkable passage in the last volume of Mr. Koestler's autobiography in which he describes an interview he had when he was travelling in Central Asia many years ago with a blind Afghan immigrant into the U.S.S.R. I will quote it in full, as it gives a first-hand account of the impact of Communism on a completely un-Westernized Asian:

> Do we all come from the same place? No——We
> come from many places and many tribes and one did
> not know of the other who was coming. Some are from

the Chilchiqs and some from Afridi and some others from other tribes. We did not know of each other, but of the new religion and of the chasing away of the Beys and the Mullahs everyone knew in Afghanistan. Some say it is a good thing, and some say it is a bad thing, but they all speak about it, although it is forbidden.

No, I could not read, even when I had eyes, but I took much thought when I heard about this new religion—for I had much time to think during the famine, though it is forbidden to speak about these sacred matters. And now I will tell you the result of my thinking:

A fertile womb is better than the loveliest lips.

A well in the desert is better than a cloud over the desert.

A religion that helps is better than a religion that promises.

And this secret which I found will spread over there where we come from, and more and more will understand it and follow our way.

But others will stay where they are and embrace the new religion and preach it to the ignorant.[1]

There is no reason to doubt the genuineness of this report and it shows convincingly how a completely anti-religious secular ideology may take on the aspect of a new religion and may compete successfully with the established faiths of the ancient East. And it succeeds not because of its ideological truth but because of its immediate appeal. It is a new gospel in the elementary sense—good news of salvation here and now.

This appeal is not so strong in the West, because the situation here is so much less simple. The distinction between religion and politics is much more obvious and we are less inclined to accept the enormous claims of the totalitarian state as a matter of course. Nevertheless the success of the totali-

[1] A. Koestler, *The Invisible Writing* (Boston: Beacon Press, 1954), p. 135.

tarian ideologies in Germany and Central and Southern Europe has been sufficiently formidable to show that we are not immune to indoctrination and that in Western Europe also there are plenty of people who desire certainty and authority more than freedom. Certainly there is no doubt that the old nineteenth century liberal ideology has become generally discredited and is no longer the ruling faith of our civilization.

Where then does Christianity stand today? At first sight the prospects seem highly favorable, for its old enemy, the antireligious secularism of the liberal rationalists, has lost its power and its new enemy, the antireligious ideology of the Communists, has not yet taken its place. There is a spiritual vacuum and Christianity seems the only spiritual form that can fill it.

Now if Christianity was embodied in a living culture, as it was in the past, or if it was the living faith of modern Western culture, there is little doubt that it would be able to take advantage of this opportunity. But the situation is not so simple as this. For centuries now there has been a divorce between Christianity and Western culture which has led to that process of secularization to which I referred at the beginning of this chapter. This has not destroyed our religion but it has left it in a position of weakness and social isolation. No doubt the Communists attack Christianity as the ally of the capitalist system, but in actual fact no such alliance exists. Christians are isolated between two rival forms of secularism, one of which is openly hostile while the other is indifferent or negatively hostile. In fact Christians are fighting a war on two fronts, each of which requires its own tactics and strategy.

The conflict with Communism (and the other totalitarian ideologies also) is by far the easiest to understand, owing to the fact that their opposition to Christianity is clear, consistent and complete. They have a creed and a dogma, they have an ideology and a social philosophy, and a code of ethics and moral values. Finally they form a secular church, a community of believers with its own very highly organized hierarchy of institutions and authorities.

But the other and liberal form of secularism has none of these characteristics. It does not possess any formulated creed and its *raison d'être* is to be undogmatic and anti-authoritarian. There was a time—two hundred years ago or rather less, during the period of the Enlightenment—when Freemasonry attempted to create a sort of liberal Church, but the attempt broke down about the time of the French Revolution and since then liberal secularism has been an unorganized and amorphous movement. Nevertheless it does possess a sort of ideology and social philosophy and a set of moral ideals if not a consistent system of ethics. In the past this liberal ideology and moral idealism has exerted a very powerful influence on the Western mind, and though its principles are now regarded as platitudes they continue to be repeated on a thousand platforms and in hundreds of thousands of publications, so that they have become part of the democratic way of life, something in the atmosphere which millions of men inhale every day when they read the newspapers or partake of political discussions.

This is a difficult situation for Christians to deal with. They know where they are when they are faced with the aggressive challenge of Communism, but they have no clear idea of where they stand with regard to this other type of secularism. They are quite ready to join with their fellow citizens in democratic states to affirm their allegiance to general principles like the Four Freedoms, yet when they do so they are using the same words in a different sense. There is an unresolved misunderstanding on general principles. I think it is true to say that the average English or American Christian shares the general atmosphere of modern secularized Western culture and feels no difficulty about it until he is suddenly brought sharply up by some concrete issue, such as religious education, contraception, divorce and so on.

The result is that the secularist regards the Christian as illiberal and intolerant. Possibly the best known example of this secularist reaction is the work of Mr. Paul Blanshard and his comparison of Catholicism and Communism as two different forms of totalitarianism. Of course, if it is totalitarian to claim authority over the whole of human life, then Christianity is totalitarian and so are all the other world religions. But this is a misuse of terms, for totalitarian is essentially a political concept and implies a totalitarian state, whereas the fundamental distinction which Christians make between Church and State and spiritual and temporal authority is the opposite of totalitarian and is perhaps the only ultimate defense of man's spiritual freedom against the totalitarian challenge and the growing pressure of the secular state. And this is especially true of the issue with which Mr. Blanshard is concerned. For in claiming the right to maintain separate schools and to teach its own principles to its own people, the Church is the champion of freedom in the most vital matter, and even the liberal democratic state is becoming totalitarian when it asserts the principle of the single school and claims a universal monopoly of teaching.

It is in this field that the secularist danger is most formidable. In politics Christianity can accommodate itself to any system of government and can survive under the most severe forms of despotism and autocracy. And in the same way, it is not bound to any economic system and has in the past existed and expanded in a world of slavery as well as in a world of freedom, under feudalism and capitalism and state socialism. But if it loses the right to teach it can no longer exist. The situation was entirely different in the past when most people were not educated and when church and chapel provided the only channel of popular instruction. But today, when the whole population of every civilized country is subjected to an intensive process of schooling during the most impressionable years of their lives, it is the school and not the church that forms men's minds, and if the school finds no place for religion, there will be no room left for religion elsewhere. It is no accident that the introduction of universal compulsory state education has coincided in time and place with the secularization of modern culture. Where the whole educational system has been dominated by a consciously antireligious ideology, as in the Communist countries, the plight of Christianity is desperate, and even if there were no persecution of religion on the ecclesiastical level, there would be little hope of its survival after two or three generations of universal Communist education. Here however the totalitarian state is only completing the work that the liberal state began, for already in the nineteenth century the secularization of education and the exclusion of positive Christian teaching from the school formed an essential part of the programs of almost all the progressive, liberal and socialist parties everywhere.

Unfortunately, while universal secular education is an infallible instrument for the secularization of culture, the existence of a free system of religious primary education is not sufficient to produce a Christian culture. We know only too well how little effect the religious school has on modern secular culture and how easily the latter can assimiliate and absorb the products of the religious educational system. The modern Leviathan is such a formidable monster that it can swallow the religious school system whole without suffering from indigestion.

But this is not the case with higher education. The only part of Leviathan that is vulnerable is its brain, which is small in comparison with its vast and armored bulk. If we could develop Christian higher education to a point at which it meets the attention of the average educated man in every field of thought and life, the situation would be radically changed. In the literary world something of this kind has already happened. During my lifetime Christianity has come back into English literature, so that the literary critic can no longer afford to ignore it. But the literary world is a very small one and it does not reflect public opinion to anything like the degree that it did in Victorian times. The trouble is that our modern secular culture is sub-literary as well as sub-religious. The forces that affect it are in the West the great commercialized amusement industries and in the East the forces of political propaganda. And I do not think that Christianity can ever compete with these forms of mass culture on their own ground. If it does so, it runs the danger of becoming commercialized and politicized and thus sacrificing its own distinctive values. I believe that Christians stand to gain more in the long run by accepting their minority position and looking for quality rather than quantity.

This does not mean that Christianity should become an esoteric religion for the learned and the privileged. The minority is a religious minority and it is to be found in every class and at every intellectual level. So it was in the days of primitive Christianity and so it has been ever since.

The difference is that today the intellectual factor has become more vital than it ever was in the past. The great obstacle to the conversion of the modern world is the belief that religion has no intellectual significance; that it may be good for morals and satisfying to man's emotional needs, but that it corresponds to no objective reality. This is a pre-theological difficulty, for it is impossible to teach men even the simplest theological truths if they believe that the creeds and the catechism are nothing but words and that religious knowledge has no foundation in fact. On the other hand I do not believe that it is possible to clear the difficulty away by straight philosophical argument, since the general public is philosophically illiterate and modern philosophy is becoming an esoteric specialism. The only remedy is religious education in the widest sense of the word. That is to say, a general introduction to the world of religious truth and the higher forms of spiritual reality.

Now the Christian world of the past was exceptionally well provided with ways of access to spiritual realities. Christian culture was essentially a sacramental culture which embodied religious truth in visible and palpable forms: art and architecture, music and poetry and drama, philosophy and history were all used as channels for the communication of religious truth. Today all these channels have been closed by unbelief or choked by ignorance, so that Christianity has been deprived of its means of outward expression and communication.

It is the task of Christian education at the present time to recover these lost channels of communication and to restore contact between religion and modern society—between the world of spiritual reality and the world of social experience. Of course this is not what is commonly meant by education, which is usually confined within the narrow limits of schools and examinations. But instruction cannot achieve much unless it has a culture behind it; and Christian culture is essentially humanist, in as much as there is nothing human which does not come within its sphere and which does not in some way belong to it.

Thus Christian culture is a very rich and wide culture: richer than modern secular culture, because it has a greater spiritual depth and is not confined to a single level of reality; and wider than that of any of the Oriental religions because it is more catholic and many-sided. For the average modern man, however, it is more or less a lost world and one from which even the modern Christian has been partially estranged by his secular environment and tradition. Consequently Christians have a double task: first, to recover their own cultural inheritance, and secondly to communicate it to a sub-religious or neo-pagan world. I do not believe that the second of these is as difficult as it appears at first sight, because people are becoming more and more aware that something is lacking in their culture; and there are many who are still far from positive religious belief but who possess a good deal of intellectual curiosity about religion which may become the seed of something more.

Apart from the Communist and dogmatic secularist, there exists a growing consciousness of the inadequacy of rationalism, alike as a philosophy of life and as a method of education. The influence of modern psychology above all has made men realize that their behavior is never entirely determined by rational motives, and that the power of enlightened self-interest—and even of class interest—is far less extensive than the nineteenth century believed. Hence we are no longer satisfied with an education which confines the mind entirely to the sphere of rational consciousness, which cultivates the intelligence and starves the emotions, which ignores the existence of the unconscious forces in psychological life and concentrates its attention on the surface activity of the mind. For such an education inevitably produces an internal schism in personality and culture which is ultimately disastrous. Sooner or later the forces that have been ignored and repressed take their revenge and destroy the rational unity of the personality and the culture by their violent eruption into the sphere of consciousness.

It is true that the psychologists themselves have had their own form of rationalism and materialism which has led them to concentrate their attention on a single aspect of the unconscious—the repression of the sexual impulses—and to neglect the rest. But this is easy enough to explain, since modern psychology began as a form of individual psychiatry and was not primarily concerned with the problems of society and culture. But it is impossible to understand these social problems in terms of the Freudian dualism between unconscious impulse and rational consciousness. Human life—and especially the life of man in the higher cultures—involves three different psychological levels. There is first the sub-rational life of unconscious instinct and impulse which plays such a large part in human life, especially the life of the masses. Secondly there is the level of conscious voluntary effort and rational activity which is the sphere of culture, *par excellence*. And finally there is the super-rational level of spiritual experience, which is the sphere not only of religion but of the highest creative forces of cultural achievement—the intuitions of the artist, the poet and the philosopher—and also of certain forms of scientific intuition which seem to transcend the sphere of rational calculation and research.

Now in the past all the great civilizations of the East and the West have recognized this world of spiritual experience as the supreme end of human culture in general and of education in particular. It is only during the last two centuries that Western man has attempted to deny its existence and to create a completely secular and rationalized form of culture. For a time the experiment succeeded, but only so long as it was carried on by men who had been trained in the tradition of the old humanist culture and who accepted its moral values and intellectual ideals with almost religious conviction.

But as soon as this minority culture gave way to the rule of the masses, with the coming of universal education and universal suffrage and universal mechanization, the new secular culture proved unable to control the sub-rational forces which are always present below the surface of culture. During the present century these forces have manifested themselves in a succession of revolutions and wars which have steadily increased in violence and destructiveness until they endanger the existence of Western civilization itself.

The true cause of this phenomenon is neither political nor economic, but psychological. It is the direct result of the one-sided rationalization of modern culture and of the starvation and frustration of man's spiritual nature. In reality the conflicts of human nature and society cannot be solved either on the material or on the rational plane. The divergent forces of unconscious impulse and rational purpose can only be reconciled by the subordination of both of them to a higher spiritual principle.

For the third psychological plane which I have mentioned— the plane of spiritual experience and religious faith and intuitive vision—is also the center of unity for man and society. It is here that a culture finds its focus and its common spiritual ends; and here also is the source of the higher moral values which are accepted not merely as rules imposed by society for its own welfare but as a sacred law which finds its tribunal in the human heart and the individual conscience.

In the last resort every civilization depends not on its material resources and its methods of production but on the spiritual vision of its greatest minds and on the way in which this experience is transmitted to the community by faith and tradition and education. Where unifying spiritual vision is lost— where it is no longer transmitted to the community as a whole —the civilization decays. "Where there is no vision, the people perish."

This vital element in human life has been denied or forgotten during the triumphant expansion of modern secular civilization during the last century. It is only by the rediscovery of this lost dimension of culture and by the recovery of man's spiritual vision that it is possible to save humanity from self-destruction. This is the real task before modern education— a task so great and so different from what men have been ac-

customed to look for from education that there are many who
will deny that it is possible. Yet there can be no doubt that in
the past, not only in Europe but in every great civilization,
the higher forms of culture were always orientated toward this
ideal of spiritual knowledge, and there were few who would
have denied that the true object of education was the cultivation of man's spiritual faculties.

However at the present day the very success of our civilization in terms of material wealth and technical achievement has
led modern culture further and further from its spiritual center
and has destroyed our sense of spiritual community. This divorce of culture from its spiritual foundations is the malady of
our age and it may well be fatal to the society which gives way
to it completely. Nevertheless there is no reason to believe that
the disease is inevitable or incurable. The deeper levels of the
human consciousness have not been lost by the changes of the
last one hundred and fifty years; they have only been obscured
or overlaid by surface activities. The time has come for a
movement in the reverse direction—a movement from the cir-
cumference to the center—which will restore the lost balance
between the outer world of mechanized activity and the inner
world of spiritual experience.

It seems to me that the time has come when the universities
should consider whether it is not possible to do more for Christian studies. The Christian culture of the past was an organic
whole. It was not confined to theology; it expressed itself also
in philosophy and literature, in art and music, society and institutions; and none of these forms of expression can be understood completely unless they are seen in relation to the rest.
But under existing conditions this is impossible. One can study
some parts of the whole in detail but never the whole itself.
To understand the development of Christian culture it must be
studied in all its three major phases—Ancient, Medieval and
Modern; Patristic, Scholastic and Humanist; Byzantine,

Gothic and Baroque.[2] At the most it is possible to study one of the first two parts of these triads in isolation from the rest, while the third cannot be studied at all. The result of this situation is that we tend to view Christian culture exclusively in one of its phases only. Thus the men of the nineteenth-century Catholic revival saw it exclusively in its medieval phase, so that they identified Christian culture with medieval culture, and especially with the culture of the thirteenth century, while others have followed the same course with the culture of the Patristic age. And the effect has been to narrow our whole conception of the subject so that we fail to see how it transcends the limitations of any particular age or social environment.

Of course it may be objected that the subject is too vast a field to be studied as a whole. But the same may be said more or less of any great culture—such as Hellenism or Islam or the civilization of China—yet in those cases any specialized study of the past must be accompanied by a general study of the whole.

This gap in our education caused by the absence of any systematic study of Christian culture is now more and more being recognized by the specialists themselves. In a recent American survey on the place of religion in higher education sponsored by the American Council of Education, the writer of the section on Music, Paul E. Langer, asserts:

> The great problems underlying the relation of art and religion are seldom touched upon in the literature of the subject. As a rule most writers confuse religious thought and its manifestations in art with the mere existence of church music. . . .
> Many writers, even those excellent in the technical aspects of their field, echo the somewhat naïve popular

[2] But each of these phases is further divisible into two ages as I have shown in detail in Chapter 3.

conceptions of the utter decadence of the Church of
Rome during the High Renaissance. Nothing is said
about the Catholic Reform, of the thousands of great
religious paintings, masses and motets that were produced in profusion during this supposedly godless era.
And nothing is said about the manner in which the old
church met the challenge of the new, the artistic effects
of the Counter-Reformation, the role of the Jesuits, etc.
The regenerated force of Catholic dogma, the first artistic affirmation of the Counter Reformation that are
summed up in the work of the Palestrina, are recognized but not explained.

These criticisms were made with particular reference to *The
Oxford History of Music*. But the same criticism could be
made in every field; above all in history, where a great standard work like *The Cambridge Modern History* ignores the
whole subject of Baroque culture. No doubt things are better
today than when the Cambridge volumes were first published.
The tide of opinion has changed, but even so the general
study of Christian culture is ignored both in university curricula and by educated opinion at large. Until this has been
changed, the secularization of modern civilization will go on
unchecked. Christians can only react successfully through cultural and educational channels and they are unable to do so
unless they possess either their own institutes of higher education or reasonable opportunities for the study of Christian
culture within the existing system.

It is true that Christians do not always recognize this. There
are many who look on Christianity and culture as alien from
one another and who regard the world of culture as part of
"this world," the world that lies in darkness under the domin-
ion of evil. In their extreme forms such views are irreconcilable
with Catholicism. Nevertheless there is a kind of Catholic
Puritanism which separates itself as far as possible from secular

culture and adopts an attitude of withdrawal and intransigency. Now this attitude of withdrawal is perfectly justifiable on Catholic principles. It is the spirit of the Fathers of the Desert and of the martyrs and confessors of the primitive church. But it means that Christianity must become an underground movement and that the only place for Christian life and for Christian culture is in the desert and the catacombs. Under modern conditions, however, it may be questioned if such a withdrawal is possible. Today the desert no longer exists and the modern state exerts no less authority underground in the subway and the air raid shelter than it does on the earth and in the air. The totalitarian state—and perhaps the modern state in general—is not satisfied with passive obedience; it demands full co-operation from the cradle to the grave. Consequently the challenge of secularism must be met on the cultural level, if it is to be met at all; and if Christians cannot assert their right to exist in the sphere of higher education, they will eventually be pushed not only out of modern culture but out of physical existence. That is already the issue in Communist countries, and it will also become the issue in England and America if we do not use our opportunities while we still have them. We are still living internally on the capital of the past and externally on the existence of a vague atmosphere of religious tolerance which has already lost its justification in contemporary secular ideology. It is a precarious situation which cannot be expected to endure indefinitely, and we ought to make the most of it while it lasts.

And I believe that it is the field of higher education that offers the greatest opportunities; first on the ground of economy of effort, because a comparatively small expenditure of time and money is likely to produce more decisive results than a much greater expenditure at a lower level. And secondly because this is the sphere where there is most freedom of action and where the tradition of intellectual and spiritual freedom

G

is likely to survive longest. Moreover the need for action is especially urgent in this field, because the social changes of the last half century have extinguished the old tradition of independent private scholarship to which these studies owed so much in the past. But today the disappearance of the leisure class makes this kind of unorganized individual scholarship impossible. Either the church or the universities must carry on the tradition and make themselves responsible for the maintenance of these studies or the work will not be done at all.

As I have pointed out elsewhere, every turning point in European history has been associated with a change in education or a movement of educational reform. We are today in the presence of one of these turning points of history and consequently the time is ripe for a new movement of educational reform.

This reform can be conceived in two alternative ways. On the one hand it can be seen as a return to the tradition of Christian education which has always been one of the main sources of Western culture and which still remains today as the representative and guardian of the spiritual tradition in our civilization. On the other hand it can be seen in terms of psychology as a movement to bring modern education into closer relation with the psychological bases of society and to re-establish the internal balance of our culture.

But these two alternatives are not in contradiction to one another. They are rather two different aspects of the same process. It is necessary to extend the range of modern education not so much in width as in depth, and the obvious way to do this is by a better understanding of the Christian tradition as the spiritual source and the moral basis of our culture.

7
Christianity
and Western Culture

THE SURVIVAL OF A CIVILIZATION DEPENDS ON the continuity of its educational tradition. A common educational system creates a common world of thought with common intellectual values and a common inheritance of knowledge, which makes a society conscious of its identity and gives it a common memory of its past. Consequently any breach in the continuity of the educational tradition involves a corresponding breach in the continuity of the civilization; so that if the breach were a complete one, it would be far more revolutionary than any political or economic change, since it would mean the birth of a new civilization, or at any rate the death of the old one.

I do not know how far these facts are generally admitted, or whether they would be regarded as a platitude or as a paradox. Certainly I do not think that modern opinion fully realizes the immense antiquity and persistence of the great educational traditions. Perhaps it is easier to see this in the case of the more remote and alien civilizations than in that of our own, for example in the case of China where the continuity of the Confucian tradition of education and learning has always impressed the Western observer. But I do not think we give sufficient consideration to the parallel phenomenon of the tradition of liberal education in Western culture which is practically as old as the Confucian tradition in China and which has played such an essential part in forming the mind and maintaining the continuity of Western civilization. Only the specialists in classical studies (and by no means all of them) realize the full significance of that great tradition which had its origins twenty-four centuries ago in ancient Athens, and which was handed down from the Latin rhetoricians to the monks of the West, from the medieval church to the humanists of the Renaissance, and from the humanists to the schools and universities of modern Europe and America.

The failure to recognize the importance of this element of educational tradition in our civilization is the more serious because everywhere today civilization is being subjected to the growing pressure of revolutionary forces which threaten it with complete disintegration. In the East, above all in China, the issue is a comparatively simple one. There the tradition of an ancient and intensely conservative culture has been violently interrupted by the sudden invasion of a new political order, a new social system and a new ideological doctrine, all of them closely related to one another.

But in the West the situation is a much more complicated one. Western culture has never rejected change as such. It has given birth again and again to critical and revolutionary movements and it has been strong enough to overcome them and even to profit by them. And so our problem is not that of an alien invasion but rather of an internal revolt and a schism between the divergent tendencies in our own culture.

What makes the present situation different, and more serious than in the past, is that European civilization is suffering from a sense of discouragement and a loss of faith in its own values, such as we have never experienced before.

Now it must be admitted that this reaction is neither incomprehensible nor unjustifiable. For more than a century Western man was inspired by a boundless faith in the absolute superiority of Western civilization and in its inevitable progress to higher and higher stages of social perfection. It was only during the lifetime of the present generation that these utopian hopes have been suddenly dissipated by the bitter realities of the two world wars and their sequel. It is true that these disasters have been mainly political and economic. There is little real evidence that the internal resources of European culture, in science and literature and intellectual activity, have declined in the catastrophic way in which the intellectual culture of the classical world declined during the later centuries of the Roman Empire.

No doubt the nineteenth-century faith in Western civilization and progress was so largely based on material considerations of wealth and power and external expansion that it was not fitted to cope with the situation which has arisen from Europe's sudden loss of her position of world hegemony. But the disillusionment caused by the present crisis of European culture is not confined to a reaction against the nineteenth-century idolatry of material progress; it also affects the permanent values of Western culture and extends to the even more fundamental tradition of Western Christendom. To some extent this is the inevitable result of the sudden extension of the Western democratic ideology to peoples who in other respects possessed a totally different tradition of culture. The old nationalisms were the children of Europe. They all shared the same background of Western culture and Christian moral traditions. But the new nationalisms of Asia and Africa have no such common background. They belong to different cultural worlds—some, like China and India, of immense antiquity and complexity; others, like the peoples of Africa and Oceania, only barely emerging from the darkness of barbarism, but all eager to claim cultural as well as political equality in the new cosmopolitan society of nations.

There is a tendency in the present day to extend the demo-

cratic principle from politics to culture. As men are equal in
the democratic state, so the peoples should be equal in the
international organization of the new world, and if the peoples
are equal then their cultures must be equal also. Hence any
claim on the part of the ancient world-cultures to possess a
tradition of universal validity represents a kind of cultural
imperialism which is no less unpopular than the military and
economic imperialism of the Great Powers. In its extreme
form this idea of "cultural democracy" is obviously inaccept-
able. We cannot regard the culture of a particular Melanesian
people or even the Melanesians as a whole as in any sense
equivalent to the culture of China or India. Nevertheless the
tendency to cultural relativism is just as strong among the
scholars who have made a lifetime's study of the problems of
civilization. We see a striking example of this in the case of
Dr. Arnold Toynbee, whose whole work is based on the principle of the philosophical equivalence of cultures and who rejects the idea of the unity of civilization as a one-sided
simplification of history due to the pride and provincialism of
Western historians. The unification of the world by Western
civilization is a fact that he does not deny, but it is a purely
technological achievement which is entirely independent of
cultural and spiritual values. In the new world-unity all the
great historic spiritual and cultural traditions will have equal
shares. As he writes in a striking passage of his Creighton
lecture of 1947: "our own descendants are not going to be
just Western like ourselves." They are going to be heirs of
Chinese philosophy as well as of Hellenism, of Buddhism as
well as Christianity, heirs of Zoroaster and Mohammed as well
as of the Hebrew prophets and the Christian apostles.[1]

Thus Dr. Toynbee's historical relativism is not limited to the

[1] On "The Unification of the World and the Change in Historical
Perspective," reprinted in Civilization on Trial, pp. 62–97.

material and political aspects of culture; it extends even more explicitly to its spiritual traditions. His doctrine of the philosophic equivalence of the different world civilizations is carried further to the theological plane and seems to involve the spiritual equivalence of the different world religions.

Now it is obvious that Christians cannot accept this historical relativism when it is carried into the sphere of theology. But is it any more acceptable on other intellectual levels? Philosophy and science also involve objective intellectual values and it is difficult to see how these are to be reconciled with a thoroughgoing historical relativism which leaves no room for any judgment of values as between different civilizations.

It seems clear that we must look for some middle way between the blind faith of the nineteenth century in the superiority of Western culture and the scepticism regarding the ultimate values of Western culture which result from the relativist view of the philosophic equivalence of cultures. From this point of view it is instructive to consider the views propounded by Cardinal Newman in Dublin almost a century ago in his inaugural lecture on "Christianity and Letters" which is the first of his "Discourses on University Subjects."

In this lecture Newman states in the most unequivocal form his belief in the unique value of the Western tradition of culture. After speaking of the multiplicity of human societies and the apparent chaos of the ebb and flow of history, he goes on:

> But there is one remarkable association which attracts the attention of the philosopher, not political nor religious, or at least only partially and not essentially such, which began in the earliest times and grew with each succeeding age, till it reached its complete development, and then continued on vigorous and unwearied, and which still remains as vigorous and unwearied as ever it was. Its bond is a common civilization; and

> though there are other civilizations in the world, as
> there are other societies, yet this civilization, together
> with the society which is its creation and its home, is so
> distinctive and luminous in its character and so utterly
> without a rival upon the face of the earth, that the as-
> sociation may fitly assume to itself the title of Human
> Society and its civilization the abstract term "Civiliza-
> tion."[2]

At first sight this may seem a typical example of the nineteenth-century liberal attitude toward European culture with
its belief in the unilinear continuity of social progress and its
uncritical acceptance of its own standards and values as uni-
versally valid. The remarkable thing is that it comes from a
man who was the lifelong adversary of liberalism, and who
fully realized the fallacies of the creed of secular progress and
the deceptive character of the material power and prosperity
of the modern Western civilization.

Moreover he does not identify the great central tradition
of human civilization with Christian civilization or even with
the tradition of Christendom. For he goes on to speak of
Christianity as the second great social tradition of humanity,
analogous to and to a certain extent parallel with the first, but
possessing its own independent principles of life and law of
development. So that while these two associations are never
exactly coincident, they occupy approximately the same field
in space and time and have continued to co-operate with and
react on one another throughout the course of their histories.

Now if I understand Newman's thought aright, he believes
that his analogy of Christianity and Western civilization is no
accident but a part of the providential order of history. The
inchoate world community of Western culture provided the
natural preparation and foundation for the diffusion of the

[2] *Idea of a University,* p. 251, cf. the whole passage, 250–54.

new spiritual society in which the human race was finally to recover its lost unity. It is this Christian philosophy of history that underlies the whole of Newman's doctrine on education. And in fact nothing shows more clearly the relation between these two traditions both in their theoretical independence and their practical co-operation than the history of Christian education. It was the union of the classical tradition of human letters—as represented by the liberal arts—with the Christian tradition of religious doctrine—as represented by the faculty of theology—which gave birth to the European universities. More than that, it was the dominant factor in the formation of Western thought and one which no historian of European philosophy or literature or culture can afford to disregard for a moment.

This then is Newman's conclusion: The two traditions are different in origin and operation but their

> heir and successor is one and the same. The grace stored in Jerusalem and the gifts which radiate from Athens are made over and concentrated in Rome. This is true as a matter of history. Rome has inherited both sacred and profane learning—she has perpetuated and dispensed the traditions of Moses and David in the supernatural order, and of Homer and Aristotle in the natural. To separate their distinct teachings, human and divine, which meet in Rome, is to retrogress; it is to rebuild the Jewish temple and to plant anew the groves of Academus.[3]

Newman's theory has been described by a distinguished Catholic educator as "a philosophy of severance." The passage that I have quoted shows how unjust this criticism is. For, more perhaps than any man of his generation, Newman stood for the principle of unity in education, in religion and

[3] *Ibid.*, p. 265.

in culture. It is true that today no one can ignore the schism in Western educational and intellectual traditions. In that sense perhaps we are all of us "philosophers of severance." For the separation which Newman condemned had already taken place and has been going further and deeper ever since. First the liberal arts were separated from theology by the secularization and religious divisions of modern culture. The Reformation rebuilt the Jewish temple and the Renaissance replanted the groves of Academus. Secondly the science of nature took the place of theology as the queen of the sciences or rather as Science in the absolute sense. And finally the liberal arts themselves have been ousted by the growth of a new series of technical disciplines which have reduced higher education to a jungle of competing specialisms.

Newman saw the first and second phases of this process and he makes a very interesting parallel between the temporary dethronement of the arts by theology in the thirteenth century and the utilitarian and scientific reaction against classical education which was characteristic of nineteenth-century liberalism. What he did not foresee was that science itself was destined to be dethroned not by a revival of humanism but by the emergence of political ideology as the final authority in the sphere of education and culture. The new totalitarian ideologies have nothing in common with either the Christian or the humanist traditions but they are also no less opposed to that disinterested pursuit of knowledge and truth which inspired the scientific movement of the past three centuries. They regard education as a general technique for influencing human behavior, and science as a series of special techniques which must be strictly subordinated to the economic and military plans of the State.

Now this totalitarian demand for the political control of science and education finds its natural allies in the modern instrumentalist view of science and the disintegration of higher education into a mass of unrelated specialisms. Since the social importance of science and education has steadily increased while the cultural leadership of Christianity and humanism has diminished, it was inevitable that some other power should be called in to provide the directive element which modern technology itself cannot supply. And where was this power to be found except in the State?

Thus totalitarianism only accentuates a tendency to political control which is inherent in the nature of technological civilization. Even in Western democratic society, which consciously rejects the totalitarian solution, the element of state control and political direction inevitably tends to increase, owing to the fact that the State has taken the place of the independent organs of culture as the paymaster and controller, first of universal public education, and eventually of higher education and scientific research. Hence it is not surprising that some leading representatives of democratic educational theory, like the late Professor Dewey, go as far as the Communists in their subordination of education to the needs of the political community. In Professor Dewey's view the function of education is not to communicate knowledge or to train scholars in the liberal arts: it is to serve Democracy by making every individual participate in the formation of social values and contribute to what he calls "the final pooled intelligence" which is the democratic mind.

No doubt Dewey's democratic community is not so crudely political as that of the totalitarian ideologies. What he has in mind is not the political organization of the state but the community of popular culture. But it is no less fatal to the traditional concept of culture since it reverses the natural relation between the teacher and the taught and subordinates the higher intellectual and moral values to the mind of the masses. It is indeed difficult to see on these principles how any of the higher forms of culture could ever have arisen. For even the most primitive and barbarous peoples known to us achieve Dewey's ideals of social participation and communal experience no less completely by their initiation ceremonies and tribal dances than does the modern democratic education-alist with all his elaborate programs for the integration of the school with life.

The original founder of democratic educational theory, Jean-Jacques Rousseau, who was more consistent than his descendants, might not have objected to my criticism since he believed that civilization was rather a mistake and that the human race would have been better without it. But the mod-ern democrat, like Professor Dewey, usually has a whole-hearted and naïve faith in the value of modern civilization, and he wishes to accept the inheritance of culture while re-jecting the painful process of social and intellectual discipline by which alone that inheritance has been acquired and trans-mitted.

The Christian educationalist who does not share these demo-cratic illusions, but who equally rejects the totalitarian sim-plification that reduces culture to a political instrument, is therefore faced with two very definite problems: how to main-tain the unity of culture in an age of technical specialization, and how to preserve the tradition of Christian culture in an age of secularism.

No doubt the two ancient traditions of Christian theology and classical humanism still remain but they have themselves become specialized studies which are confined to a compara-tively small minority, and they no longer dominate the uni-versity and the whole system of higher education as in the past. Yet some unifying study is absolutely necessary if higher education is not to be entirely disintegrated into an inorganic mass of technical specialisms.

This need has been strongly felt in recent years in the United States where the development of specialization and utilitarian vocational courses has proceeded further and faster than in Europe. In some American universities there has been for many years now a course in contemporary culture which is compulsory for all freshmen. But I do not feel that a course of this kind really provides the unifying principle that we need. Where a civilization has lost its internal unity, as ours has done, it also loses its intelligible unity and the field of study becomes practically unlimited. For example the two volumes of sources which are the textbook for this course at Columbia University amount to more than two thousand pages and they include such diverse material as the Bull *Unam Sanctam* and the Communist Manifesto, Magna Carta and the Weimar Constitution, St. Augustine's views on Original Sin and William James's views on pragmatism; the Hat Act of 1732 and *Quadragesimo Anno*. No first-year student can possibly absorb such a pabulum. It needs a lifetime to digest it. And the same difficulty stands in the way of all attempts to find the necessary principle of unity in an encyclopedic subject like World History or the History of Science.

The success of the old classical education was largely due to the fact that it limited itself to a single cultural tradition and was able to study it thoroughly. Nevertheless, as we have seen, the classical tradition was not the only unifying element in Western culture. The tradition of Christian culture is even more important and reaches far deeper into the European consciousness. For it is this and not science or humanism which was the spiritual bond that transcended the divisions and antagonisms of race and class and nationality and created that society of peoples which was the community of Western Chrisendom.

Why has this essential factor not received more recognition in our educational system? No doubt to some extent it is due to the tendency of modern historians to concentrate their whole attention on the development of their own national traditions, both political and cultural, and to ignore or to take for granted the existence of that wider spiritual community out of which the national cultures have sprung. But this is a comparatively recent phenomenon, and the source of the difficulty is much older. It goes back at least four hundred years and has its origin in the one-sided classicism of the humanist educators who treated the previous thousand years of Western culture as a kind of cultural vacuum which educated men could afford to ignore.

But to do this is not only to ignore the value and achievement of Christian culture, it is to destroy the intelligible unity of Western civilization. For it is only in the light of this unbroken tradition that we can understand the nature of Western unity and the spiritual forces which have influenced and enriched the life of all the peoples of the West.

Now it seems to me that it is in the study of this unjustly neglected tradition that we can find that unifying principle which modern education requires. Unlike the new encyclopedic studies of which I have spoken, it is a manageable subject with a clearly defined field of study. Unlike the old discipline of classical studies, it has a direct relevance to the modern world and to the needs of men today. For although the old order of Christendom no longer exists, we Christians are not a negligible minority, and every Christian, whatever his special vocation and technique, has a general interest in the Christian past and a common responsibility for the preservation of the inheritance of Christian culture.

The main objection to such a solution is that it is impracticable, owing to the vagueness of its terms of reference and the width of its field of study. But as I have said, it is far less vague and indefinite than the new encyclopedic subjects like "modern civilization" or world history which have been actually introduced into university curricula.

No one denies the existence of Christian history, Christian

philosophy, Christian literature and Christian institutions. And though these have never been studied as part of an integrated whole in the same way as classical history, philosophy and literature have been, there is no reason why they should not be.

In fact the lack of an integrated study of this kind makes the detailed study of any particular aspect of European culture extremely difficult. For example it is impossible to understand the development and interrelation of the different European vernacular literatures unless we have studied the common Western tradition of medieval Latin culture by which all the early vernacular literatures were so deeply influenced. This has been fully demonstrated by Dr. E. R. Curtius in his very important book on *European Literature and the Latin Middle Ages* which was published in 1948. And if his conclusions are not more widely known and have not made a deeper impression on educated opinion, this is because there can be no public for such works so long as the study of Christian culture is nobody's business and finds no place in the curriculum of the modern university.

Nevertheless, it is difficult to exaggerate the educative value of such a study. It opens new avenues of approach to the civilization of the ancient world in which Christianity was born and to the civilization of the modern world which, however secularized it may be, still retains an organic relation to the Christian past. And between the two there stands not the cultural vacuum of a Dark Age of medieval barbarism but the historic reality of Christendom as a social and cultural unity.

The more deeply the student penetrates into this great religious and cultural unity the more aware he will become of the essential continuity of Western civilization and of the spiritual dynamism and fecundity of the Christian tradition.

No doubt the development of an integrated study of this kind involves the co-operation of scholars and specialists in many different fields. But the same is true of the old classical education. The school of Litterae Humaniores, which dominated university studies at Oxford so long and so effectively, was itself a most comprehensive study, since it covered the cultural development of the ancient world from Homer to the age of the Antonines and involved a comparatively thorough study of ancient philosophy and history as well as literature.

It is no more difficult in principle to conceive of a unified study of Christian culture which would include Christian philosophy, Christian literature and Christian history, studied in close relation with one another. In both cases the field of study comprises three successive cultural epochs[4]: first the period of formation—the Homeric age of Greece and the Patristic period of Christian culture; secondly the classical age—the fifth and fourth centuries B.C. and the twelfth and thirteenth centuries A.D.; and thirdly the age of transmission and diffusion— the Roman Hellenistic period in the ancient world and the age of the formation of the vernacular literatures and cultures in Western Europe.

From the traditional humanist point of view it will perhaps seem absurd and shocking to regard the great centuries of the Middle Ages as the classical age of our culture. But the more we study Western culture as a whole the more impossible it becomes to accept the valuation of Christian culture which has been the orthodox view of the educated world since the Renaissance. The age of St. Thomas and Dante is more central and more universal than the age of Leo X and Luther or than that of Descartes and Corneille or that of Locke and Dryden. And I think historians are more and more coming to realize the eccentric and one-sided character of the Renaissance theory of culture.

Far more serious however are the practical objections to a

[4] See note 2, p. 95.

study of Christian culture such as I have suggested. I fear it must be admitted that the introduction of a new basic integrative study of this kind is not practical politics. Modern education has become such a vast and highly organized system that the teacher is not as free as in the past to choose his own path—at least that is the case in England and, I believe, on the Continent. Nevertheless we can at least hold it in mind as a goal for the future and attempt to direct and co-ordinate our studies in this direction. In any case I believe that it is impossible to overestimate the importance of this problem, for it is only by some such study that we can overcome the schism between religion and culture which began in the age of the Renaissance and Reformation and was completed by the Enlightenment and the Revolution. This schism is the great tragedy of Western culture. It must be solved if Christian culture is to survive. And the survival or restoration of Christian culture involves not only the fate of our own people and our own civilization but the fate of humanity and the future of the world.

H

8

Is the Church
Too Western?

DURING THE LAST FOUR OR FIVE CENTURIES,
the expansion of Christianity in the non-European world has
been associated with the expansion of Western colonial power.
The missionaries went hand in hand with the European ex-
plorers and traders and conquerors who sailed unknown seas
and discovered new continents or found new contacts with
ancient peoples; indeed to a great extent the missionaries were
themselves the pioneers in the work of discovery. Consequently
it was inevitable that the peoples of the Far East and Africa
and the island world of the Pacific should have seen Christianity as something essentially Western, as the religion of the
foreigners, the Sahibs in India, the Hairy Barbarians in China
and the White Man in Africa and Oceania. And so it is not
surprising that the rise of the modern nationalist movement in
Asia and Africa with its slogans of anticolonialism and anti-
imperialism, and the reassertion of the traditions of oriental
culture against the West, should be accompanied by a reaction against the influence of Western missionaries and often
against Christianity itself. As a rule this reaction has not been
a violent one like that which produced the great persecution
of the Christians in Japan in the seventeenth century. It has
been political and cultural rather than religious. It has been
directed mainly against proselytization and education by for-

eign missionaries, but it has also led to a demand for a strictly national organization of oriental Christianity and its emancipation from all forms of Western or external control, as we see in the report of the government commission on Christian missions in Madya Pradesh, which proposed that all the Christian Churches in the region should be fused in a single national or provincial body which would be completely autonomous.

Now it is obvious that proposals of this kind are irreconcilable with the fundamental principles of Catholicism. If nationalism—whether in the East or the West—denies the right of the Church to exist as a universal autonomous spiritual society, it is a challenge to the law of God and the kingship of Christ. But this does not mean that the Church is essentially Western. On the contrary, the same principle that forbids us to make the Church a national organization also prevents us from identifying it with a particular civilization. The mission of the Church is essentially universal and it is common to all nations and races—to those of the East equally with those of the West.

We must however distinguish between this ideal universality and the practical limitations imposed by history on the circumstances of the Church's apostolate. By the nature of the case, the missionary is in some sense a stranger to the nation and the culture that he evangelizes. He comes from outside bringing a new doctrine and initiating men into a new society. But however supernatural is his mission, he is a human being who has been born and educated in some particular society and brings his own cultural traditions with him, and hence in some degree his native habits and prejudices. In this sense it is true the missionary tends to be too Western, so that it is his duty to divest himself of his natural prejudices and become assimilated to an alien environment and culture. As he must translate the Christian Gospel into a new language and speak with strange tongues, so too he must learn to think in terms of an alien culture and accept its social standards and values.

Yet this is not the real point at issue. For when men talk, as they do today, about the Church's being too Western they are not thinking of this inevitable but accidental dependence of the missionary on his particular cultural background; they mean rather that the Church herself has become occidentalized: that her philosophy and theology, her liturgy and devotion have been so deeply influenced by fifteen hundred years of association with Western culture that she has become estranged from the Oriental world and no longer speaks to it in terms that the peoples of Asia can understand.

Before we consider what grounds there are for such an assertion it is necessary to determine what we mean by the word "Western." On the one hand there is our modern Western civilization, which has spread so rapidly through the world during the last century. This civilization is indubitably Western, since it owes its distinctive features to the revolutionary changes which originated in Northwestern Europe and North America during the last two centuries. On the other hand there is the ancient tradition of the Catholic Church, which may also be described as Western, in so far as it is the tradition of the Western Church and looks to Rome, the ancient metropolis of the West, as its center and head. Nevertheless it is also a universal tradition, since it first arose at the point where East and West met and it derived its inheritance from them both. And if we look at the Catholic tradition in detail we shall see how this duality runs through all the different aspects of its life.

The Church itself, though it bears a Greek name, Ecclesia, derived from the Greek civic assembly, and is ordered by the Roman spirit of authority and law, is the successor and heir of an Oriental people, set apart from all the peoples of the earth to be the bearer of a divine mission.

Similarly the mind of the Church, as expressed in the authoritative tradition of the teaching of the Fathers, is neither Eastern nor Western but universal. It is expressed in Western languages—in Greek and Latin—but it was in Africa and Asia rather than in Europe that it received its classical formulation. Greek theology was developed at Alexandria and Antioch and in Cappadocia, while Latin theology owes its terminology and its distinctive character to the African Fathers—Tertullian, Cyprian and above all St. Augustine.

While these men wrote in Latin, it was not the Latin of the Romans; it was a new form of Christian Latin which was developed, mainly in Tunisia, under strong Oriental influence.

And the same is true of the new Christian Latin poetry and of the Latin liturgy itself. No doubt the Roman rite which has outlived and absorbed the other Latin rites bears an indelible mark of the Roman spirit in its simplicity, its severity and its concision. But this does not mean that it is only adapted to the worship of modern Western man, or that its spirit is alien from that of the East. On the contrary it gives it a classical, universal and supertemporal character which is accentuated by its music, which is so remote from the modern West. For what has the Mass to do with Western culture? It is the eternal offering of an eternal priesthood—"without father, without mother, without genealogy, having neither beginning of days, nor end of life, but like the Son of God, continuing a priest for ever" (Heb. 7:3).

It is impossible for us to understand the Church if we regard her as subject to the limitations of human culture. For she is essentially a supernatural organism which transcends human cultures and transforms them to her own ends. As Newman insisted, the Church is not a creed or a philosophy but an imperial power, a "counter Kingdom" which occupies ground and claims to rule over those whom this world's governments had once ruled over without rival. But if the Church is an objective social reality she is not bound to conform herself to cultural divisions. She can take whatever forms and institutions she needs from any culture and organize them into a new unity which is the external expression of her spirit and the organ of her mission to the world. If this is the case, the question we have to ask is not whether the particular elements of this unity are derived from East or West—but whether they are fit instruments of the Church's supernatural purpose. If so, they entirely transcend the sphere of political nationalism and national culture.

Let us take the case of a typical Catholic institution—a religious Order for example. Here the original institution of Christian monasticism was of purely Oriental origin and came into existence in the Egyptian desert in the fourth century. Almost immediately, however, the Church accepted this new way of life as an essential expression of the Christian spirit and spread it East and West from the Atlantic to the Black Sea and the Persian Gulf. And as it grew it adapted itself to the life of the different peoples amongst whom it came, though it remained fully conscious of its origins and of the continuity of its tradition.

It was, however, in the West that this development of monasticism produced the most remarkable fruits. It was here, in the course of the Middle Ages, that there arose the idea of the religious Order as a specialized organ of the Church, dedicated to the performance of some particular spiritual task— preaching or study or the care of the poor and the sick, or the redemption of captives. Since these Orders are specialized some of them are more adapted to one culture than to another, and it may well be that an Order that has been founded to fulfill some special task in medieval Italy or modern America is "too Western" for India or China. But this is not necessarily the case. The essential principle of the Western religious Order has become part of the common tradition of the Church and is capable of being applied to the special circumstances of the East, no less than the West.

There is therefore no need to undo the work of the Christian past and to attempt to create a new type of oriental monasticism modeled on Hindu or Buddhist patterns, for East and West already coexist in the tradition of Christian monasticism, and the same tradition can bear new fruits wherever it is planted. The vital point is not the nationality or the cultural background of the founders but the timeless ideals of prayer and contemplation and the universal spirit of the apostolate for which they are founded.

This I think is the secret of the whole matter. The Church as a divine society possesses an internal principle of life which is capable of assimilating the most diverse materials and imprinting her own image upon them. Inevitably in the course of history there are times when this spiritual energy is temporarily weakened or obscured, and then the Church tends to be judged as a human organization and identified with the faults and limitations of its members. But always the time comes when she renews her strength and once more puts forth her inherent divine energy in the conversion of new peoples and the transformation of old cultures. At no time can we expect this work to be unopposed, for the very fact that the Church represents something entirely different—the intervention of a supernatural principle and the coming of a divine Kingdom—must inevitably arouse the fierce opposition of all those human societies and powers which claim absolute power over man and refuse to admit a superior or rival. One of the strongest and most aggressive of these forces in the modern world is nationalism, and here Christians cannot expect to avoid a conflict. But the conflict is not really one between East and West: it is the old conflict between the spiritual and temporal powers, which was formerly confined largely to the Western world and has now emerged as a burning question in the East, largely owing to the introduction of the political ideologies of the West into Asia and Africa. But East or West, it is basically the same conflict, and alike in East and West the Church stands neither for East nor West but for the universal spiritual society which is destined to embrace them both: "And the nations shall walk in the light of it: and the kings of the earth shall bring their glory and honour into it" (Apoc. 22:24).

INDEX

Africa, 82, 101–102, 114–115, 117
(*See* Asia for topics)
Age of Justinian, 51
Age of the Fathers, *see* Church history, second age of
Ancient civilizations, 62, 78, 80
Anthropology, 32, 60, 61
Apostolic Age, *see* Church history, first age of
Arnold, Matthew: his criticism of Christianity and culture, 21, 22; ideal of culture, 23
Asia: Communism in, 82–83; reaction against liberal ideology in, 81; nationalism in, 101–102, 114–115; as source for Christian culture, 117–119
Athanasius, St., 51
Augustine, St., 20, 50, 51, 109, 117

Baillie, John, 44; quoted, 45
Baroque culture, 56, 95, 96
Basil, St., 50
Bede, 52
Benedictine monasticism, 74–75
Berdyaev, Nicolas, 78
Blanshard, Paul, his comparison of Catholicism and Communism, 87
Boileau, Nicolas, quoted, 66
Boniface, St., as agent in consolidation of Western Christendom, 52
Bunyan, John, 24
Burke, Edmund, 18
Byzantine civilization, 50, 51, 53
Byzantine Orthodoxy, compared with Western Catholicism, 73

Calvin, John, 43, 44, 66
Cappadociah Fathers, 50, 51
Carolingian Empire, 52, 53
Catholic monarchies, decline of, 56
Catholic mysticism, development of, 56
Celtic Church, 74

Charles the Great, importance of Empire of, 52–53
Chesterton, G. K., 65, 66
Chinese culture, 34, 35, 99–100
Christian civilization, 31–46; average man's objection to, 44; defined, 32, 33, 36; rejection of, 43; revival of, 45, 46
Christian culture, 13–30, 32, 33; compared to classical culture, 112; as culture of hope, 64–65; decline of, 22; defined, 14; epochs of, 47–59, 76, 94–95, 112; historical process, 66, 67, 73, 80; ignored in the schools, 96; influence of moral and spiritual values of, 36; inseparability of culture and religion, 68; Kierkegaard's attack on, 68–69; liberal education and the study of, 110–113; lost channels of communication, 90; monasticism in, 73–75, 118–119; movement toward, 29; need for study of, 76, 77, 94–98, 110–111, 112; of the past, 90; secularization of, 81, 85, 86, 87, 92; tradition of, 109, 110; in the United States, 40, 41
Christian education, 87; cause of schism in, 70, 71; formative elements of, 105; present task, 90, 93, 94
Christian institutions, 36, 74–75, 118–119
Christian socialists, 21
Christianity: in contemporary world literature, 89; as cultural force, 63, 64, 65, 70, 72; cultural tradition of, 29; as dynamic source of social change, 77–78; Eastern and Western traditions of, 116–118; expansion of, in non-European world, 114–116;